THE SECRETS OF PERSONAL DEVELOPMENT

ADRIAN VALLACE

THIS BOOK IS DEDICATED TO ALL OVERACHIEVERS AND HIGH-PERFORMANCE PEOPLE, FOR WHOM PERSONAL DEVELOPMENT REPRESENTS A CHERISHED LIFESTYLE.

IN THIS BOOK, I WILL SHOW YOU HOW TO BECOME DISCIPLINED, OVERCOME PROCRASTINATION, UNDERSTAND UNCONDITIONAL LOVE, AND TAP INTO YOUR FREEDOM.

Acknowledgments

I would like to express my sincere gratitude towards Louise, my wife, who had the patience to be by my side every step of the book, remaining calm even when I got impatient and felt like giving up. Thank you from the bottom of my heart for putting up with me and helping me along the way, both emotionally and with your managerial skills. Your support kept me from drifting.

I want to thank my best friend Emanuel, with whom I started my personal development journey, almost ten years ago. Thank you for always keeping me on my toes and supporting me on my journey of never giving up. All those workshops, seminars that we used to attend together, and all the books read alongside this amazing friendship have been and remain a healthy, happy, and fulfilling chapter in my life.

Many thanks to my sister Monica and her husband Adrian, who has been helping me since my mom left when I was 11 years old. There were many years in which they supported me financially, I don't think it was too easy for them. She assumed the role of mother without hesitation. I would like to thank my other sister Cristina as well, for supporting me. I will forever be grateful to my brothers and sisters, for taking me into their home and supporting me financially until I became independent. Because without their financial support, I would have most definitely ended up somewhere completely different in this life. Thank you for the emotional support, because being the youngest child sometimes comes with a burden, one I was perhaps not aware of, but I am sure that they wanted to "kill" me at least a few times after creating all those troubles, as a young kid.

I would like to offer my deepest gratitude to someone who I like to consider my mentor, the person who laid down the path of personal development for me. Even if he died over two thousand years ago, he had a massive impact and positive influence on me. I am talking about Marcus Aurelius, the Roman emperor. Everything he ever wrote is in alignment with my values. His writings on life virtues will resonate with my heart forever. It has been one of my greatest honours to have met you in a past life, and if that didn't happen, it will be an even greater honour to meet you in another life.

I would like to thank all the personal development and self-help book writers from around the world, people who have led me to this amazing journey. This book would not suffice to mention all their names, but I am forever and deeply grateful to all those humans out there that are striving to make this world a better place, with their books, workshops, seminars and everything else that helps us live in harmony together on Mother Earth.

And last, but not least, I would like to give thanks to anyone who has encounter me during this lifetime, whether we were work colleagues or college mates, and any other relationships that I have been in, as thanks to them, I have managed to grow and evolve, in one way or another. Whether it was an emotional lesson or any other life lesson, I bow to the divine in anyone who crossed paths with me in this lifetime. Thank you.

Eleven life-creating secrets for an abundant and prosperous life

1 Mind, body, and spirit.

2 Unconditional love.

3 Faith, belief, and willpower.

4 Education.

5 Discipline.

6 Learn how to reward yourself.

7 Persistence and motivation.

8 The ABC of financial awareness.

9 Opportunities and actions.

10 Virtues, respect, and values.

11. Legacy.

ABOUT THE AUTHOR

My name is Adrian Vallace, and I am a yoga teacher, as well as a writer. One of my life's purposes is to become the greatest version of myself through my work. I would love to be able to help as many people as possible, to achieve their dreams and goals. When it comes to my own person, the thing I focus the most on is a life of freedom. I am just a spiritual being living yet another human experience, someone who started this life in an unconscious state of being, and a child of two parents who eventually broke up, shortly after I turned four. Now I am becoming the highest version of myself, trying to help anyone who resonates with me and wants to evolve in life. Right now, I'm at a place in my life where I feel extraordinary. I am living off grid, I am immensely grateful for everything that I am and everything that I have. I feel fulfilled because I have the time to follow my dreams of becoming the greatest version of myself. How do I become this person I dream of? Through personal development such as yoga teaching, building personal development courses, writing books, and self-love, as well as taking care of my family and my lovely pack of dogs.

However, it hasn't always been like this as I grew up in a poor family. We were so poor that we didn't even have a fridge in the house, not to mention food, and I was wearing my sister's clothing, as she was older than me. My parents split up when I was around four years old, then two years later they got back together for a short time, thinking that everything is going to be okay, but they only managed to pull it through for another six years. Then, my mum decided to sell the flat and left without any notice, leaving us on the street. Suddenly, we were homeless. That happened without my dad knowing, as the flat was in my mother's name, she had inherited it from her own mum. One day, she decided to somehow just leave, without any notice or at least saying goodbye. Abandoned for the second time, I kept asking my dad where mum was. He was at a loss for answers, he knew just as much as I did.

A few days went past, and I started looking for her on the streets of the city, late at night. I was only ten, wandering at night around the city, scared and brave at the same time, hoping that I would find her. It was hopeless. I would come back home and sit on the radiator by the window. We used to have those old cast iron radiators, and I would cry terribly whilst gazing out the window, hoping that I'll see her through my tears. My dad went to the police and the press at that time, telling them that she was missing. On the fourth or fifth day, a reporter came around the house to interview us, and find out if anything had changed. Maybe he thought he could help us find her. My dad kept thinking that something bad happened to her.

However, almost a week went by, and after looking and asking about her around the neighbourhood and then the entire city, we were sitting in the living room talking about her. At some point, we heard a key turning in the front door, then my dad jumped and asked who was there. It was a middle-aged man asking us what we were doing in his house. Dad grabbed a stick and a knife, telling him to go away, but he insisted that he would call the police, which he eventually did. He then locked the door and we put a sofa in front of it, so it won't open so easily. After about one hour had passed, the police knocked at our door, shouting at us to open the door. Dad replied, "what the fuck do you want". The policeman said that the house belonged to the respective man and how he had bought it from a woman. He showed us the contract agreement. Dad opened the door, and the policeman said that we have twenty-four hours to leave the flat, otherwise there would be more trouble, as if that was what we were missing at the time.

    We scattered around the house to see if we could find any money. I think we found some, around the value of ten pounds, in an old box filled with photographs. There was no other option but to sleep on the street, under the stairwell of our old building, while my dad was desperately looking for a place to live. He wasn't working at the time, so we had it hard for a while, sleeping on the street and all. The amount of shame from my friends, children with whom I was going to school with, was increasing exponentially. They were walking past us, going to school every morning, pointing their fingers at me. By then, they all had seen me in the newspaper, I was a superstar, if you can call me that. Apart from the shame, the amount of guilt was tremendous, not to mention the fear.

    I remember how scared I was when the people from the orphanage came to pick me up. I have vivid memories of how they told my dad "We've come to take him into foster care". Dad looked at me and asked me if I wanted to go with them, as he didn't have the power to look after me. We had no house, no food to eat. I remember grabbing him by his leg as strongly as I could, and then telling him that I don't care, I will eat what you eat, if there's nothing, I will eat nothing, but I don't want to go with them. And so, I stayed with him until he found a place to live in the countryside, where I grew up, thanks to him and my elder sisters, to whom I am forever grateful.

    So, my journey as an adult started when I turned eighteen years old. I left the country in search of a better place, where I could make more money and live a better life, because in a third world country it's harder to thrive, especially financially. But as the time went by, I developed addictions and bad habits, which went on for years. No surprise there, looking back at my childhood. Until one day, when I realised that I am in trouble and that I will not go anywhere if I drink alcohol at nine in the morning and sniff cocaine at twelve noon on a Monday. In addition, I was always in debt, dealing with a negative financial situation. That was the day when I looked at myself in the mirror and understood that my life needed to change, right then and there!

    Now, I am experiencing financial freedom and I'm heading towards financial abundance. And I am very grateful for the fact that I have discovered personal development about eight years ago. Since then, my life has improved, especially through the power of discipline. Everything in my life shifted, with better health, better relationships, better finances. Looking at my past, there is no way I will ever go back. Reading self-help books has improved my mental health, allowing me to oversee the control panel of my life, especially with my ADHD brain. This is one of the reasons I am writing this book now, in the hope that it will guide others, just like I have been guided. I've started meditating and doing yoga. These are two amazing tools, which improve my everyday health and balance, helping me evolve in my spiritual journey. The knowledge that I've gained from within has helped me raise my level of consciousness, making me more aware of what's happening within and around me, and I am able to stay present more often. If you are suffering from an attention disorder, like me, then you know how important this is. I've gained happiness and fulfilment, and I've disciplined myself a little bit.

Now I am an amazing time manager, which means I can very easily create and guide personal development programs. Every person on this planet has an amazing story that would benefit the world and I would love to hear it. I was born in Romania, in 1990. My parents gave me a wonderful name, Adrian. From the age of twenty-five, I have started to my personal development journey. I have read books and practiced what I learned. At that age, I was procrastinating a lot, up to a level where I was always in serious debt and my mind lacked the power to focus on a better future. I was always drinking, smoking, and crying, asking myself why I didn't have a better life. Basically, I was victimising myself, instead of assuming responsibility for my actions. If you feel the same, that's one of the reasons you picked up this book, either from a shelf or online. It's because it resonates with your gut instinct.

Those irresponsible actions were hurting me, family, friends, girlfriend, colleagues, and others around me. So, if you find yourself in the same position and have the strength to recognize that you too, like plenty of others out there, are procrastinating, let me congratulate you first, because not everybody has the willpower to do so. Inside this book, you will find extraordinary methods, meant to not only lift you back up, but to help you become the greatest version of yourself. It contains real life experiences and exercises that you can put in practice, observing the results with your own eyes.

Now, I am a certified yoga teacher and a cognitive behavioural therapist, and I love to help people to resurrect, restore, regain, and develop some of the most important plans of their life, with implications for relationships, financial aspects, emotional journey, physical health, etc. I live in the southeast of Romania, near the sea, in a lovely city called Constanta. Here is where I am a student of life. I decided to write this book out of self-love, as well as frustration, because these two emotional states have a great motivating influence, even if they mean two different things and they can instigate one to excel and prosper in life, as you will see in the next couple of chapters.

I wrote it out of love for the community, and my fellow human beings, who find it hard to live every day on this planet, for all the people who struggle every day because they didn't have a chance to a better life, or because of their situation, or didn't have any guidance, some didn't have parents or mentors, or healthy surroundings as children. I am more than sure that we all desire a better life, one that is healthier, more fulfilled. You do too, amazing being and wonderful reader, otherwise you wouldn't have bought this book, which by the way makes me feel fulfilled, because I know that it will guide you in the direction that you want to go.

Let me explain the frustration part. I was born like most people, poor and traumatised, without a parent and then both between the ages of four and six, and then from the age of eleven, as well without a house. At the age of eleven, I became homeless, with my father. We slept under the staircase of the block of flats, in plain view of our neighbours and friends for some time, at some of his friends' workplaces, and in the schoolyard, until my father found a place in a village. I lived there until I turned eighteen. We rented different places, and my father used to pay the rent by working around the house. That's how it worked back then, you couldn't just find a job on social media or online. We were lucky, because my older sisters helped us, sending money each month from abroad, money my father used to buy food and send me to school. We ended up homeless because my mother had sold the apartment and left us. I don't know the reasons for her actions and I'm not going to dwell on them.

I can only draw some conclusions, but that is not healthy. Therefore, I will abstain, with the understanding and wisdom that everything happens for a reason. Anyhow, now I am at an age where I am deeply grateful for everything that I am and have, and I do not blame either of my parents for what has happened in the past. I am deeply grateful to them, because they gave birth to me, raised me and took care of me the way they knew best. Thank you, mom, and dad. Frustration continued to accumulate in my lifetime, as I was observing myself working all the time for someone else. Nothing good was happening to me as a result, so I was angry, crying all the time, pitying myself.

I felt frustrated that I didn't have enough money to buy my freedom, something every person on this planet is by universal law entitled to. Until one day, when I discovered that everything that I want and do is completely my choice. We all have the inner power to become what we want, we have an inner mine gold deep within us, which wants to be released and set us free, so we can become happy and fulfilled in every area of our lives.

With this book, I don't want to promise or sell you anything, because I know that we are attacked everyday with all kinds of commercials, on how to become the wealthiest, the prettiest, the healthiest, and so on. But I strongly believe that if you're willing to apply what I am about to share, you will be able to obtain and achieve everything that you want. To put it in the words of my mentor, Marcus Aurelius, "being able to transform every obstacle into materials". In this book, you will learn how to become disciplined whereas the financial aspect, psyche, emotional balance, spiritual aspect are concerned. You will discover how to stop procrastinating for good.

I am not writing this book as a Band-Aid for your wound, but to teach you how to heal yourself, despite your past, status, sex, race, or wherever are you in this world. But for you to achieve this, you must promise yourself one thing, and that is you truly have a desire to change for your own good. Promise yourself that you will commit to the process of personal development with your entire being, otherwise you will not gain anything, as information without practice offers no benefits, like you already know. I am certain that once you have purchased this book, a big part of you wants a change for the better. So, I suggest that you keep your mind and spirit open, so that you can achieve the best results. I wish you good luck on your own path to personal development. Now, let's unleash the eleven creative secrets for an abundant and free life.

CHAPTER 1

MIND, BODY, AND SPIRIT

In this chapter, we will discuss techniques and learn how to balance ourselves, to attain harmony and balance within our life.

MIND

"The mind is everything. What you think you become." (Buddha)

So, let's begin with the human mind, which is one of the most powerful tools that we have, since the discovery of fire and the wheel. The brain is the most complex organ of the human body, and it has many functions, such as keeping us alive, controlling the breathing and the circadian rhythm. The cerebellum or the reptilian brain helps us to keep our balance and use our five senses. However, I will not dwell much on that, I will rather focus on the subconscious part of our brain. My desire is to show you how to tap into the subconscious, to teach you the techniques we can apply for a balanced mind. The truth is that we live over eighty percent of our lives being controlled and pushed to act, according to the emotions and patterns that have been programmed into our subconscious mind.

The subconscious mind is like an iceberg. Imagine that the conscious mind is the twenty percent at the surface, which includes a little bit of willpower, the short-term memory, a bit of logical and critical thinking. The remaining eighty percent is taken over by the beliefs, patterns, imagination, intuition, the long-term memory, emotions, and habits, so imagine trying to tap into all of this every day, without being conscious or aware of your behaviour and how you actually think and behave.

Do not think that tapping into these parts will be simple. In the process, you will discover hidden traumas and other experiences. These shaped you in a way that might not resonate with your thinking, therefore creating a troubled mind, unacceptable for the fragile human ego. However, you must trust the process of evolution and love and accept yourself just the way you are, because you are perfect in the eyes of universal creation.

Let's start off easy with some simple meditation techniques, which are going to ground you and keep you present. You can always start with a comfortable position, sitting cross-legged, on a chair if your knees won't allow you, or you even lay down on your back on the bed or sofa. The most important thing is to keep our spine straight because that's where most energies are blocked. In yoga, they say you are as young as your spine. Now take five breaths, inhale through the nose and exhale through the mouth. Continue with ten strong breaths, inhale through your nose and exhale through your mouth. Try to lock your throat and breathe through your diaphragm, so that you can hear your breath like the ocean waves. This is called the *ujjayi* breath and it will help you find inner balance.

After the ten breaths, just breathe calmly in and out through your nose, with ease, so that nobody else can hear you breathing, not even yourself. You will be able to do it in time with practice. Then try to meditate for at least fifteen minutes if you are a beginner and try not to think of anything. It is only normal that various thoughts will start popping in our minds, therefore with every thought that comes along, let go of it, focusing on your breath, on that split second break between your breaths. Or think of them as balloons that disappear into the sky. Do this meditation for twenty minutes, and always remember that you are not your thoughts, just the one who sees them, an observer. Do not attach yourself to them.

After you finish, find a few positive thoughts to repeat in your mind as a mantra or be grateful for the things in your life, for the things that happened for you today. Do not fall prey to the false belief that there isn't anything to be thankful for. be grateful just because you woke up today and you can breathe. Now this is just the tip of the iceberg when it comes to meditations and breathing techniques, this is just to balance your mind and give you a head start for the day.

There are many meditations that you can find to balance your energy channels, the ones that I suggest the most are mindfulness or za-zen like the Buddhist call it, energy balancing with chanting for chakras, love and kindness, and body scanning. I will explain them here, the first one that we already did earlier, za-zen or a "no thoughts meditation" is best done in the morning when our mind is in a theta wave state, which means that our mind is in a slow activity, therefore it will not produce many thoughts for our morning meditation.

Now, let's explore the energy-balancing meditations. Our bodies have one hundred and fourteen chakras and seventy-two thousand nadis, which are energy channels. We will cover the seven main ones here.

Muladhara or the root chakra sits at the bottom of our spine, represents our grounding and survival instinct, and it represents an earth element. When we are meditating for the balancing of the root chakra, we chant *Lam*.

Svadisthana, the sacral or water chakra, is connected to guilt and shame and represents our lunar or moon energy, our yan, our femininity, the emotions. When we are meditating for the balancing of the sacral chakra, we chant *Vam*.

Manipura, the solar plexus, or the fire chakra, represents our decision making, the force and strength towards achieving things in life, the power of the sun. When we are meditating for balancing of the fire chakra, we chant *Ram*.

Anahata, or the heart chakra, represents the unconditional love that we are made of and which we must share. When we are meditating for the balancing of the heart chakra, we chant *Yam*.

Vishuddha, or the throat chakra, represents the truth that we speak. For its balance, we chant *Ham*.

Ajna, or the third eye chakra, represents the vision and intuition. When we are meditating for the balancing of the third eye chakra, we chant *Aum*.

Sahasrara, or the crown chakra, represents the awakening and understanding that we are one with the universe and it's our connecting channel to it. When we are meditating for the balancing of the crown chakra, we shouldn't chant. Instead, we should listen. This is best to do during the day, because it will activate the energy within your body, and you will become very energetic and active.

As for the evening or before going to bed, it is best to do body scanning meditations, for a healthier and well-balanced sleep. Breathe in and out through your nose slowly, taking each breath from the top of your head to the tip of your toes. As you follow through, if you notice any pain, that represents an imbalance and a blockage. Breathe through it, from top to bottom and from left to right, in and out, and watch it dissipate. Scan your body several times for at least twenty minutes, followed by moments of love and kindness. Here, you can think of anybody, whether you know them or not, loving and sending them kind thoughts as such: "I am very grateful and I thank my dad, from the bottom of my heart, for having raised me since I was a baby, and for always being there for me" or "thank you for the rain today", "love, abundance, and prosperity for everyone around the world" and the list is endless. Try to imagine how you open your heart and send energy to all the people and everything. Feel it, and understand that you are made of love, carrying an unlimited supply of love with you all the time. All you must do is just access it, through self-awareness and meditation.

Now, meditation is one of the first steps towards inner balance, and a pathway into our subconscious mind. We can achieve the same thing through visualisations and affirmations. Tapping represents another technique worth considering. It is also known as EFT, which translates as the emotional freedom technique, and represents an alternative therapy for post-traumatic stress disorders or PTSD, helping with the subconscious healing of fears and traumas. With tapping, you can stop smoking, lose weight, improve your finances, and live in many wonderful ways.

This is how tapping works. You have eight meridians to tap on your body. The first is directly on the top of your head; the second is in the beginning of the eyebrow; the third on the outside corner of your eyes; the fourth under the eye about one inch, on the bone; the fifth under your nose, where the middle of a moustache would be; the sixth on your chin, halfway between your bottom lip and the bottom of your chin; the seventh on the collar bone, where the sternum and first rib intersect; and the last one under your arm, where a bra strap might be, about four inches under your armpit.

You start by saying "even if I have this problem, I deeply and completely love and accept myself". So, you must tap on the head meridian, until you have said the full sentence. Move onto the second one and so on, until you have reached your armpit. Then, start over and repeat at least five to ten rounds. Be careful, as a beginner, you might start feeling a bit high or dizzy. Do not worry, these are the chemicals in your body, such as dopamine, being activated by tapping on your meridians. Just breathe normally, in and out through your nose, and you will rebalance yourself. If you are more advanced, you can do this for fifteen minutes, two to three times a day, in the morning, afternoon and evening.

Here are some real examples if you don't know where or what to start with. Even if... "I feel shy talking to this girl, I am choosing to be confident now", "I have the exam tomorrow and I feel anxious about it, but I trust myself to take it", "I smoked for forty years and feel awful, but I now chose to let go and free myself of it" ... and the list could go on. No matter what you want to change or improve in your life, keep on tapping until it changes. It usually takes up to twenty-one days, but for deeper traumas and depending on everyone's different beliefs, it may take longer.

I used to be shy or anxious when using a public restroom, going to parks, or wherever there would be a possibility of a human passing by. I have practiced tapping for two weeks and I've used a few mental affirmations and I healed myself. Maybe for some people that doesn't mean much, however, for me it represented a mental obstacle, which affected my self-esteem, bringing it to the lowest possible level at the time. I hope this technique will help you on your journey and if you require more details about it, there are books you can read and lots of content on YouTube about it, do not hesitate to do your research.

I also recommend trying cold showers, if you want to improve your immune system and become strong as a lion. Consider taking Wim Hoff's course, check out the app or YouTube channel on breathing techniques. This guy is incredible, he climbed the Himalayans only in his shorts, swims under frozen lakes, and he teaches people around the world how to improve their immune system and never get sick again. Now, whether you follow these techniques or any others, please make sure that you do them for at least twenty-one days, to get into your subconscious mind as deep as possible, thus changing and reprogramming your old beliefs.

BODY

"The body is your temple. Keep it pure and clean for the soul to reside in." (B.K.S Iyengar)

Let's talk about the amazing human body that we possess right now in this life. The body, even though it seems that it's made of a few pieces, two hands, two legs, the head, the neck and the body, is actually a single complex unity, connected through our brain and nervous system, as well as the emotions that lead us to our actions.

So, for example, I am afraid of feeling rejected. Therefore, whenever that happens, I go back to my old habits, hiding somewhere where I am alone and eating chocolate and other sweets, or smoking, which is harmful and addictive for both the body and mind. We must take conscious control over our emotions and how we feel. Imagine that you work in sales, and you are afraid of rejection, have no doubt that you will end up with an unhealthy lifestyle.

How do we take control over our lives? We spoke in the previous chapter about the mind, we can achieve this by reprogramming it, but that is not enough. We must control our emotions, and one way is by doing physical exercises, yoga, boxing, athleticism, regular training. The list is limitless, you have to find whatever resonates with you, otherwise you will give up easily. I worked out for three years in a row and I never liked lifting weights. I used to believe that type of training was annoying, tiring, and useless. Truth be told, I was only doing it to look good physically. My mind wasn't in alignment with my body, not until I discovered callisthenics. Now, I can't wait to wake up every morning and do it, with both my heart and my body, because I absolutely love it, and I will forever be grateful for discovering it.

Now each to its own, but I chose callisthenics and yoga, callisthenics for the body, and yoga for the mind, body, and spirit. Yoga helps me to keep my emotions balanced. With every suppression that we go through, we tense certain parts of our body. Yoga helps relieve the pains, tensions, and blockages throughout our bodies, and it can be done by anybody, at any age, no matter the body type, as there are versions made for everyone willing to try it.

There are so many types to discover, but the main core ones are Ashtanga Vinyasa, Hatha, and Yin yoga. Ashtanga Vinyasa is the more active of them all, a yang practice, and it requires a lot of strength, flexibility, and stamina. It can be tried by beginners, intermediate or advanced practitioners. Hatha is an easier type, where you do the poses as you feel, and can stay in your asanas "poses" as much or as less as you want. It's a practice that is very simple to follow, one which can be done by children and old people at the same time. Yin is easy, but slightly more intense, as you must keep a pose for longer periods of time. Now, if you are a fan of yoga, or would like to practise and become a practitioner, you can take my course @UNIVERSAL FREEDOM 33.

No matter the type of sport you decide to add to your lifestyle, you must keep a healthy diet as well, and drink as much water as possible. Of course, don't abuse it, in such a way that you will need to go to the toilet every ten minutes, just make sure that you are hydrated enough. If you live in Europe, where the graphics show that we consume around one two to three litres of tap water per day, I advise you not to drink from the tap, unless you have a filter. Remember when we were kids and they used to teach us in school that our bodies contain about 75% water? Not only is that true, but it's very important that we understand its effect over our bodies, for us to respect it more.

Water is an essential constituent of the protoplasm of living cells in our body, and it's involved in photosynthesis and breathing. That is why everything needs water to survive and grow, plants, trees, animals etc. Water contains memory, being recycled repeatedly, over the decades and millennia. We have countless sources of water, including the rivers, the lakes, the seas, the oceans, and the springs. We use this water not only for drinking, but also for various other activities. Water is part of a cycle, with stages of evaporation, condensation, and collection. This is our planet's recycling method, through the clouds we get it back, it doesn't leave the earth. Even though our planet is amazing and has a natural way of recycling, we still manipulate it, through sewage systems. We send it back into the rivers and seas, we have been doing this for decades, harming the whole nature with our way of life, as well as ourselves. It is wise to say that water is flexible, so we understand that not only does it contain cellular memory, but it can be changed through it.

For more details, you should read the book written by Masaru Emoto, "The Hidden Messages in Water", where he talks about his experiments, and how water is connected to human consciousness. He did some experiments, such as if you curse at the water, it will change its molecular structure, and you will feel a difference if you would drink it. And if you say that you love it, it changes again, obviously for the better. Every time you drink water, say with a good intention that you love it, and that you are grateful for every sip, and then notice the changes in your body.

At home, we have a eight litre glass barrel, from which we drink water every day. Around it, I wrote beautiful messages such as love, prosperity, abundance, harmony, unity, balance, richness, strength. We printed and put them around the barrel, with kind intentions, and I will forever be grateful to Masaru Emoto and his scientists, for discovering what I think it might be a lifesaver, because the good intention towards water can act like am inner filter, which cleanses and heals from within. We, as humans, recycle that back into the nature, so that the animals and the fishes can receive the love from us through water. I know that is a small step, but when we are evolving as a species, I think that every step matters. I hope that this little chapter about water made you a bit more interested and conscious about how it works.

Food is essential for our body, because it is true when they say, "you are what you eat". We must be very careful how much and what we eat, depending on our lifestyle. For example, if your dream is to be a bodybuilder, I am not going to say you should eat less, just healthier. But, if you want to become a yogi, you will have to eat less and healthier. Regardless of what you want to become, it is very important that you try to eat as healthy as possible, because studies have proven that heavy food affect us negatively. Our heart, blood circulation, and the overall pressure will suffer. If you eat sweets and fast food all day, not only you will die younger, but you will live in poor health for the rest of your life. Your diet can lead to the appearance of cancerous cells and to many other diseases that shouldn't have any dominion over the human body, if we are in control of our body, through our minds.

We can do that by eating as fresh as possible. Do not let any food sit in your fridge for weeks, or even months, and avoid sugar and salt. I understand that not everyone can afford eating as healthy and as fresh as possible, but at least try to cook at home and avoid takeaway meals. Try to stop eating meat for a few months, if you can't suddenly, start with red meat first for a month, then try to avoid poultry and the rest, and keep fish in your diet for a while. When you feel ready, try six months without meat, and when you want to upgrade, so to speak, go dairy free as well, and notice the difference in your body. Countless doctors, scientists, and researchers have confirmed that a plant-based diet is healthier. If you no beneficial changes are noticed, you can go back to your previous lifestyle and diet.

I am not writing this only out of compassion for animals that are being butchered and grown in the worst ways possible, only for human profit. Truth be told, they don't all act like that, probably only the big companies. The little farmer treats his animals much better than the one who grows animals on a massive scale, it must be so.

However, it is a proven scientific fact that animals feel love, that's why every mother takes care of her babies no matter the breed or type, such as cows, chickens, bears. All animals feel pain. If you were to hit a dog with a bat, that dog would cry and bark in pain. So, imagine how animals are being butchered every day for human consumption, in unimaginable ways, and as they are being hit or cut to death, all of that energy, stemming from their pain and fear, is transferred into their cells and then onto our plates. We say that is quality protein, that is absurd, I tell you, that is second-hand protein. Imagine this. A cow eats grass, and it grows up to a tonne, as a full-grown adult animal, and yet we are not capable of getting our proteins through our veggies, an average adult human male weighing around seventy to eighty-five kilos.

Broccoli has more protein than steak, and spinach alone equals the protein content of chicken and fish. I know that some people will say that plants are alive as well, but plants are living organisms, not living animals. The reason why the human body can digest plants better is because we aren't carnivores by nature, but only by habit. We needed this lifestyle to survive thousands of years ago, but that is not necessary anymore. And if you have noticed the teeth of a carnivore, such as the ones of a lion or a tiger, they are different than ours. Check the teeth of a horse or a cow, and you will notice that we have a similar teeth structure.

Plants have a lower frequency than animals, and that means a lower level on the energetic scale. Eating plants, we move slower, we think slower, and we evolve slower. As I said, I am not trying to make anyone change their eating habits, as I love everyone for what and who they are, I am just trying to raise awareness on how food benefits our body, and what steps could be taken, for our bodies to evolve easier. Before we close this chapter, we must understand that certain foods can make us addicted and harm us. Food is making millions of people sick every year, so stay present, cook, and eat fresh food, and drink plenty of water.

I have attached a picture of the human emotional and vibrational scale, starting at the bottom, with negative emotions at 20, and going up towards positive emotions, to joy or enlightenment over 700.

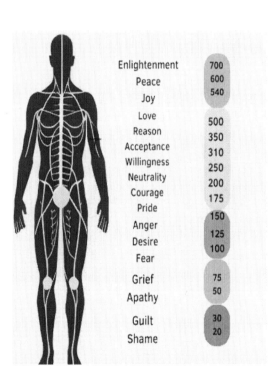

SPIRIT

"The spirit is like a candle that can never be extinguished. It might flicker, but it will always reignite." (Unknown)

We all have heard in our lifetime about souls and spirits. Basically, they are one and the same. Whether you believe in having a soul or not, let me share this little bit of wisdom with you. I believe that spirits are born within a higher dimension and that is where they start their journey, by choosing to incarnate and live on planet Earth, which is like a "hard knock" school to them. The main purpose of the spirit is to achieve *samadhi* or enlightenment, but to get there, there are levels and obstacles that it has to go through, in order to be able to learn that negative and positive doesn't mean bad and good, or hot and cold.

Our human mind, more specifically the ego developed this duality and separation due to its limited knowledge. So, the spirit doesn't have a notion of time, as the spirit world is in a dimension where time doesn't exist. Lucky them, so I say. But as it incarnates and reincarnates in this world, in human bodies, it understands what it must go through before the actual reincarnation. It selects its parents and the probabilities of life experiences, in other words, yes, the spirit knows where it comes, it makes choices to learn and evolve towards enlightenment.

For example, if a human has harsh life experiences and traumas that some other people find it impossible to live with, these are part of the progress and growth of the spirit, things that it must go through to learn. If the spirit has just begun its journey, it is harder to evolve, that comes with experience, just like in humans. The spirit reincarnates, from one life to the other, with every person who has lived, new karmic experiences are created, with the spirit working and learning from each life. Sometimes, it is hard for the body to be in alignment with the spirit because the human mind is limited, with addictions and bad habits, or to summarise, without self-love.

However, it is very important to understand that we wouldn't exist without our spirit. I will share a secret with you, so you can see that you can achieve anything through your spirit, or better said, when we align with it. If we understand why the spirit is going through this certain experience of life, this traumatic experience, or this blissful experience, then we can be aware and conscious more easily, and become one with the spirit, by taking our ego out of the way, when the spirit tries to live the experience.

Let me share an experience with you. As you might remember from the first chapter, I grew up as an abandoned child, thinking most of my young life that I wasn't wanted by my mother. Thus, I grew up with a heavy emotional baggage or trauma as the psychologists call it nowadays, therefore I hated my mum for years and years, bringing into my life nothing but emotional turmoil, acting like a victim, with low self-esteem, lots of subconscious pain, and negative patterns. But as I grew up, around the age of twenty-five, I started to practice self-love which led me to think that I should see a past life regressionist.

When I was going through past life regressions, my spirit guides revealed some of my past life experiences, and how in one of them I was a Roman warrior. That was about two thousand years ago, during Caesar's time. We were looking for freedom, that's what they were told back then. We were seeking freedom through conquering, that was Caesar's motto as well, 'MORIR INVICTUS', which means "I will die unconquered" in Latin. So, as we were looking for the so-called freedom, they were slaughtering every little child in their way.

You might have heard the stories about Caesar looking for baby Jesus, in the hope he would bring him freedom. Well, I was part of that squad, and the funny thing is that I made a vow that is still imprinted onto my body, as well as the subconscious, until the present day. Years and years ago, before I went to this regressionist, when I was about twenty-two, I had a tattoo made. It was of a wing and it was meant to symbolize freedom. Underneath it, I wrote Caesar's motto, 'Morir Invictus'. I chose Greek letters at the time, but the meaning was the same. I remember how the regressionist made me watch what my spirit guide was ready to show me, through a screen like at the cinema.

And there I was, wearing an outfit consisting of leather shorts and a vest, with a big sword in my hand, ready to cut a little baby's head off, whilst his mother was next to him or her, crying and trying to protect her child, all hope lost. I saw all that in the form of rapid images, played through my subconscious mind, and I understood that woman was my mom in this lifetime. Because I took her child away at the time, I had to somehow pay my past life karmic experience, by growing up without a mother.

After in-depth research, I discovered that back then or even earlier than that era, I had made a pact with the devil. I don't know why and how, but looking back at my history, and through my mind and thoughts, I have realised that was true and that there is no way to get rid of a contract with the devil, not an easy way at least. However, we shall talk about this in another book. In this one, I will only mention how I managed to defeat my demons and break the contract. All that energy was taken away through me. To really understand that, and not only with the mind, I had to get in touch with my heart and therefore with my spirit.

To get in touch with your spirit and align yourself with its energy, you must love yourself unconditionally. Try to evolve in all the areas of your life, so that your source of energy is unlimited and untouched by other entities, whether we are talking about alcohol, drugs, sex, any other addiction, or bad virtue. That is how the devil feeds upon your energy. Are you willing to just let go of that without a fight?

You know, I understood that we have free will one morning, when I was doing my workout in my garden and my three dogs were playing. I have two big boys, a Rottweiler whose name is Energy and a Cane Corso named Spirit, and a little Metis girl named Winter, because she is white like snow. So, she was having a go at Spirit, and he kept pushing her to the ground with his big paws. Keep in mind that he weighs about fifty kilos, and she only about ten. Whenever he would push her, she would jump a couple of feet away.

However, as I was watching them play, or better said, how Spirit was bullying her (my own perception) at the time, I was trying to decide whether I should interfere to break them up and save her. I chose to let them be, as I realized that they were following their instinct. And I stopped looking at the situation from a dualistic point of view, where good and bad exists, and judgments appear intricately. I understood that everything happens for a reason, and it's perfect the way it is. As soon as I realised that I chose free will, not interfering, they continued to play, without harming one another. Now, obviously, if they were to fight hard, I would most definitely have interfered, so that they did not end up getting hurt.

Sometimes, it can be hard to act upon our free will, this takes courage. It is also very important, if we want to carry a lighter burden. Please practice more self-love. What do I mean by that? Be grateful every day for who you are, for what you have, for your parents, for your life, for the food, for the water, for the oxygen that keeps us alive and everything else. Stop being too hard on yourself, don't judge, don't hate, and be deaf to gossip.

Now, coming back to getting in alignment with the spirit, the easiest way is through self-love. That is where the healing takes place, and you become harmonious and balanced. Your life starts shifting and all your manifestations come to life, and you become blissful, by becoming one with your spirit. Just look at the vibrational chart and you'll understand the things that you need to let go of much easier. You need to operate from the same level as your spirit, letting go of anger, fear, shame, and guilt. Instead, you will choose courage, compassion, love, peace, and joy.

Make this your lifetime practice, as nobody expects you to become enlightened and free overnight. If they do, they will be the ones to suffer, and so will you if you expect to become free quickly. There are monks who take a vow of silence, retreating into the mountains, where all they do is practise their spirituality. Unless you will follow their practice, and move into the mountains by yourself, away from the rest of the world and Western society, don't assume you will become enlightened overnight. Even the present-day spiritual masters will tell you that they need quite a few lives on Earth to reach samadhi. So, be patient and believe that you are doing the best you can, and you'll attain more freedom with each day that passes.

"The spirit is the true self. The body and mind are temporary manifestations of the spirit." (Eckhart Tolle)

CHAPTER 2

UNCONDITIONAL LOVE

"When you will be able to let go with ease, you will understand and experience unconditional love.

This a very interesting subject to talk about, and even more difficult to feel for most people. You might say no, that's not true, parents love their kids unconditionally. Such kids know how unconditional love feels like, and that's how it should be, but not every parent wants the kids he/she has. Most of them are born "by mistake", as I've heard many parents stating, and that's the cold hard truth, whether we like it or not. If something bad were to happen to their kids, and they're going to help them only because they're their parents, that's not unconditional love. That's merely a selfish act, done because of fear of judgement from the rest of the world, self-judgement, or because of their own conditioning and beliefs.

Of course, that is not true for every parent, because I know that some of them really love their kids. But if you look at the statistics for every country, almost every generation comes out with traumas, with unconditional love lacking during childhood. That is not only a parental mistake. Our spirit reincarnated in this lifetime, by choosing those parents, for the sake of learning certain lessons, and because of intergenerational trauma and past karmic experiences.

Unconditional love is when you love someone without limits, without asking for anything in return. Like this planet loves us, even though we harm it every day, by polluting and using its resources to a dead end. To attain that level of energy, first of all, you have to love yourself just the way you are, without any judgement, expectations, the need or want of becoming something that you're not. Only then you can love those around you, because how can you love somebody else, if you don't love yourself, it won't work.

The practice of self-love is one of the most amazing things that you can do in this lifetime. Take care of yourself, of the essential things in your life, the mind, body, and spirit. Practice being grateful for everything that you have and for everything that you are, as everything happens for a reason. You are living this experience so that you can learn and grow, thrive, and clear your karmic patterns. There is a deep purpose behind your life, and that is to preserve and hand down the best qualities of your parents and your ancestors to those who follow you, whilst at the same time eradicating any negative patterns that you have inherited.

The truth is that unconditional love resides within us all. Our mind wears a mask, however, which was created by our ego during our childhood, as well as the rest of our life, to protect us. This mask has harmed us more than we think. By creating such identities, we have suppressed the true nature of love that awaits within us. Just like a little kid who waits for his parents to let him go out and play. For us to do that, we must lose our hatred for one another, to let go of our desires, our pride, and our fake identity, all of which have been created by our ego.

Up to the point I turned twenty-nine, I have never experienced unconditional love, not from myself, nor from the person I was with. I had relationships where I was with that person, just because I thought it was nice to have sex, she looked sexy, I was feeling lonely, or out of other selfish reasons, such as the social status and I'm not afraid to admit all these things. I just didn't know how to love. I haven't experienced anything resembling it, until one day, when I decided to attend a tantra speed dating event.

I have to say that at that time, I was very self-aware and conscious of what I wanted. So, in a way I felt and thought that I understood what a healthy relationship looks like to me. I had even envisioned, through meditations, how the girl would look like, her features and general appearance. I wrote it all down on a sheet of paper. I wanted a dark-skinned girl, with Asian features, who knew what she wanted from life. She had to be self-aware and love herself.

And guess what, I went to the event, which was an incredible experience. There she was, this beautiful Caribbean girl with Indian roots, who was very spiritual and knew who she was. We talked about who we were and what we wanted. When she asked me what I wanted, I remember telling her that I wanted to experience unconditional love. Her eyes smiled in return, and she said that it was very kind of me. I kneeled and took her hand in mine, saying to her, "I apologise in the name of all men who have ever done any harm to you, or ever hurt you in any way, physically or emotionally".

Apparently, that was the moment that she fell for me. Later that week, we met for tea, and since then, I enjoy every single moment next to her, because she has showed me what unconditional love is all about. Within a few weeks after we have met, on our third date, we decided to take psychedelic mushrooms. She came to my place for the first time, and we agreed to share some mushrooms. It was her first try and as we eased into the trips, we saw what resided within our subconscious minds, letting ourselves be led by the wisdom of the Mother Earth.

Our higher selves started to conquer the illusions we were living in, and our ego was fading from our minds, leaving us in the sweet embrace of what I thought was a vortex of love energy. I remember she was mirroring me, as we were lying down on my yoga mat, on my bedroom floor. She asked, "so what now", to which I replied "well, right now, baby, the way I see it, I believe that everything is possible, and we are unlimited". And as we sat down, we saw these magical lands with sunshine, and us starting an amazing journey together, which we called "new beginnings".

After that, we made love, without stripping or getting naked, only through eye.

gazing, moving around in a circle, and touching each other. I must be honest, I told her this as well, that was the best love experience I have ever had. She admitted having felt the same. When the energies of our higher selves collided together, that magical moment was created. And I would never change it for real sex ever because that is how the gods make love and we have had the blessing of tapping into it.

I am forever grateful for the fact that I had the chance to be with this incredible woman, who is still in my life. And this is not the reason why we are still together. Shortly after that, we decided that it was best for us to split up, due to circumstances that we thought they would not be good for us in the future. It all had to do with some limiting belief that I was carrying at the time. No, that wasn't it.

In the day that we broke up, we were both feeling hurt and especially her, because she had never had a relationship where everything was going great, and the guy decided that it was time to go on separate ways. My decision took her by surprise, as we were having the time of our lives together. I told her that it was for the best if we were to break up at that point, before it got any harder. It was her reaction that made me understand what unconditional love looks like. When she said that she respects my decision and that she still loves me, wishing me the best in life, that was the moment when I saw the true colours of love.

If I would've been with another woman, as I have been in the past, it would have never ended in peace, not even close. And that made me think. If I let her go, then I would lose not only a girlfriend, but a true best friend and my true love. That would go against my entire belief system. I have been looking for love my entire life and now when it is knocking at my door, I am not going to let her in, just because of what other people might think or other limiting beliefs. Hell no, it's time to take a stand, because it's about my own happiness, and if I don't care, then nobody else will.

So here I was, telling her that I would love for us to experience an amazing journey together, apologising for thinking otherwise. I told this girl that I wanted her back in my life, request with which she thankfully agreed. Not long after that, I've asked her to marry me, and now we are living together in our own house, happily married. We both have the same goals and dreams, on which we work every day. As she likes to say, we are a high-performance couple. Thank you, Louise, for loving me unconditionally.

Now, I didn't know much about love as a kid because my mum didn't want me. At the age of four, my dad took me to my grandmother's house, in another city, where I grew up without the love and affection of my mum. I lived there until I was about six and a half. I developed an abandonment wound, which I carried as part of my emotional luggage throughout the years. At the time, I didn't realize what was happening, because I was too busy living in the present or playing like any other child. But as you can understand, I missed her. Nevertheless, my grandma did a great job, taking care of me as best as she knew, so thank you sweet, sweet grandma, and may you rest in peace.

My dad wasn't around much at the time because he was working in the city that we left from. I could only see him during the weekend, because he had to work hard, as he had to pay alimony to his ex-wife and their three kids, a boy and two girls, until they turned eighteen. Because he wasn't around much, I developed an injustice wound, as I felt it wasn't fair that he wasn't around. I never blamed him, instead I tried to understand his struggle as I grew up. And then, before I turned seven, my dad decided to take me back to my mum. They got back together, and I had to start school.

Their relationship didn't last long. Four years later, she sold the flat and ran away, while me and my dad moved to the countryside, where he raised me until I turned eighteen. As soon as I got my passport, I left the country.

When I said I didn't know much about love, I meant from a feminine part or point of view. That is why I wasn't very good at keeping a relationship over the years, because deep within my subconscious mind, I had this strong belief that every woman in my life will abandon me. Therefore, I would unconsciously create situations in which I was either making the woman in my life leave me, or I would think that she would abandon me anyway.

My dad filled in as a mum as well, but only as much as he could and knew. As a teenager, I remember asking him what I should do in a relationship. His answer would be "son, just use them and leave". It didn't take me long to understand that his views weren't aligned with my needs. I realized that his advice wasn't right. Nevertheless, I respect and love him, for trying to be both a dad and a mum during my childhood. He taught me what love is, through his own perception, what it means to be a good friend, and how to trust and love everybody, no matter their gender, colour, financial status, or race.

He also taught me not to fear anybody or anything as a kid. We used to play and fight. Imagine me and my dad fighting in my grandma's front garden. He used to tell me to never ever fear anything or anybody, no matter their size. That helped me to become fearless. I look at this as an act of love and I am very grateful for it. Back in his days, life was different. When he grew up, people hated each other very easily, especially if there were differences between them. In the '60s and '70s, racism represented a major issue. I thank God that he hasn't dragged that negative karmic energy with him during the years, so that he would pass it over to his kids. Thank you, dad, for teaching me to believe in equality, because this has helped me over the years, as I saw hatred and inequality unfold before my eyes.

Love can be understood and felt in so many ways, shapes, and forms. A man can feel love just by gazing at the oceanic blue sky during the day. A woman can see and feel love while watching the flower in her back garden bloom. A kid can feel it upon seeing the smile of parents or friends while playing, I know that I feel love flowing and swirling through my body after every morning meditation and prayer. I feel it every time I see my wife, and the list could go on and on, with an unlimited point of views and perceptions.

Let's get back to understanding how to love unconditionally. We can only do that by starting with ourselves, there is no other way around it. If you think that you love someone else more than yourself, that's not necessarily true love. It could mean that you abandoned yourself and are taking care of others at your own cost. Whether it regards your health, emotional status, or financial independence, it doesn't matter. You cannot drink from an empty cup, can you?

So, imagine you give all your energy to someone else. If you're drained, what's left for you? I understand that you might want to love your friends, partner, or family unconditionally. Trust me, everyone would love to help others and make this world a better place. To treat their loved ones without any judgement when they are making mistakes, show their vulnerable side, and give away their energy without expecting anything in return. But that cannot be achieved unless it has been attained from within first. That's why people fight and have arguments all the time, because they are limited to their conditioning and cannot let go with ease when someone makes a mistake.

We all make mistakes, and our harshest critic lives inside our brain. Unless we let go of it, we cannot forgive ourselves. We judge ourselves, which brings along feelings of shame and guilt. These are some of the lowest vibrational energies that we can tap into. Therefore, letting go is essential for reaching unconditional love. When we let go, we tap into compassion and vulnerability, where true power lies. So, how can we love ourselves unconditionally? Well, if you've read the previous chapters, you've probably understood that there are steps that can be taken, starting with balancing your mind, body, and spirit. The elevation or uprising of your inner and outer evolution should follow.

You know that eating healthier is a way of loving yourself, and the vessel that carries you through life. The same goes for exercising, as it has a balancing effect. Then you work on elevating yourself through meditation, reading books that expand your consciousness, and becoming more spiritual. At the end of the day, you should think about the spirit that lives in your body and attune it, to evolve as a spiritual being. Do you want to be able to love your partner, family, friends, business partners, or anybody else in this world, even strangers, without any conditions and limitations? Good! Start with yourself first.

If your relationship is a bit shaky, or you fight a lot, start respecting yourself a bit more. Learn what kind of love language you and your partner have. Maybe read a couple of books on relationships and take a course or see a therapist. Gary Chapman is a great writer; he wrote a book called "The five love languages". You can read it to discover your love language. Maybe you are the type of person who likes declarations and gifts, or you prefer the physical closeness, services offered, and time spent together. Regardless of what it is, read it or share it with your partner.

You will both discover or rediscover your love language. This is important, because if your partner loves to spend time with you, and you give him/her gifts in exchange, your relationship will suffer. Therefore, you need to understand your love language and you will see a big difference, not only with your partner, but with your friends and family, throughout your lifetime.

There are many people out there that we can learn love and compassion from, many spiritual masters such as Thich Nhat Hanh, Eckhart Tolle, or Radhanath Swami. The latter has written a book called "The journey within", which contains a story full of compassion, one that left a mark on myself. When I think of unconditional love, this story comes to my mind.

There was a little girl in India, and she was meant to marry a man much older than her. She was a teenager, and he was well in his thirties. They got married and by the time she was eighteen, she already had three or four kids, and was pregnant with another one. The latter wasn't her husband's, and when the family found out the truth, they told him to cast her out. And so, he did. He beat her up and left her in a ditch, where a cow came and stood over her, to protect her from the other cattle. She ended up in a barn, where she eventually gave birth, and found her calling and God.

Many years later, she ended up helping many abandoned and helpless children. She erected houses to protect and help the poor as well. One night, she was walking home, when she saw a man crying in a ditch. It was a rainy day, but she stopped to help him regardless. As she came closer to him, she realised that the man was her ex-husband, the one who had beaten and banished her years back. Nevertheless, she took him to the house where the kids where living and told him that she will only take care of him as a mother and not a wife. He agreed, and then she went onto telling those kids that they should give that man love, because he needs it the most.

Every time I feel angry and judgmental, I think of that story, which let's be honest has many valuable lessons to offer. That woman was a saint, she had to be, to take such actions and decisions. That's why we need to follow humans like this. I'm not saying we must become like them unless that's the purpose. Otherwise, it's a way of finding love and compassion when we are trapped by our limited beliefs and ego. One of the most powerful energetic strings that holds this planet together is the unconditional love that we experience or learn to put in practice.

The parable of the prodigal son, as recorded in Luke 15, illustrates God's unconditional love. A man's younger son asked his father for his share of the estate, packed his belongings, and took a trip to a distant land where he wasted all of his money on parties and prostitutes. About the time that his money vanished, a great famine swept over the land, and he began to starve. He finally came to his senses and realised that his father's hired men at least had food to eat. He decided, "I will go to my father and say, « Father, I have sinned against both heaven and you, and am no longer worthy of being called your son. Please take me on as a hired man. »"

While he was still a long distance away, his father saw him coming and was filled with loving pity. He ran to his son, embraced him, and kissed him. I think that the reason he saw his son coming while he far away was that he was praying for his son's return. He spent a lot of time each day watching that lonely road on which his son would return. Even as the son was making his confession, the father interrupted to instruct the servants to kill a fattened calf and prepare for a celebration – his lost son had repented; he had changed his mind and had returned to become part of the family again. God demonstrated His love for us before we were Christians, but this story proves that God continues to love his child who has strayed far from him.

This biblical story teaches us that God loves us unconditionally. So what does that mean? Well, if the source of universal energy – God, Yahweh, Buddha, Allah, or whatever name you would like to assign to it – if its unconditional loving energy runs through our veins, why can't we, why shouldn't we, or why don't we do love ourselves unconditionally, when that energy resides within each one of us? We have lost our ways and have fallen into the trap of this ''doing and becoming era''. We've lost our connection and have become imbalanced, due to our negative habits, greed, fear, jealousy, and hatred for one another.

We are not connected to this planet anymore as we used to. We aren't walking barefoot on the ground anymore. We are wearing eight types of clothes on us to protect us from the people and the weather, which instead of protecting us, it's making us weaker. We are hiding away from the sun, as we have been tricked into believing it is bad for us. We have been warned that looking directly at the sun will make us blind, but the truth is that gazing at the sun enhances our pineal gland and our intuition. If the sun has a negative effect over us, then how come that everything in this world – plants, flowers, trees, veggies, animals – need sunlight for growth?

Have you noticed how dandelions are coming out when there is a sunny day and how they close back in a cloudy day? We have been lied to for so long, that not only it became our reality, but one of our biggest fears as well. We do not go out in the snow naked anymore, because we have been told that we are going to catch a cold or come down with the flu. If we train and regulate these exposures, the opposite will happen. Our immune system will strengthen, our self-esteem will increase, and our nervous system will function better, all of which are essential to counteract emotional imbalances, so often seen in this century.

I know this might seem far-fetched, but do you think that during the palaeolithic time period, cavemen wouldn't jump in a cold lake to get fish, just because it was frozen? They certainly did, otherwise they would have starved. I am not saying that we should go and hunt fish in frozen lakes. I would like for people to understand that cold water immersion and walking barefoot in the park can have a grounding effect. Such activities can restore our lost connection to Mother Earth, helping us rediscover the unconditional love we have for ourselves and for each other.

Nobody can take that away from you. Throughout history, it has been proven how unconditional love overcomes anything and anyone, countless of times. I remember being a naughty teenager and stealing money from my dad. When I returned the next day, with the tail between my legs like a puppy that chewed one's favourite pair of shoes, he gave me a ''fatherly look'', and then asked me if I was hungry. He asked me to sit at the table, asking where I was and what I have been doing, without any judgement.

He has grown old and it's time to return the favour, so to speak. Whenever he comes home drunk from the pub, I can either scold him, or look at him with compassion, understanding his situation. His behaviour is directly related to his traumatic history. If I should try to change his ways, then I am going to become a selfish person, someone who doesn't love him unconditionally. And I will turn into somebody with expectations, who doesn't accept him the way he has chosen to be.

Of course, I believe in having boundaries, and so should everybody, because it's for their own benefit. Otherwise, kids will be walking around the streets or on the playground with knives, and grownups would no longer respect each other. If healthy boundaries are maintained, and we allow space for mistakes, love can flow endlessly. Think of a boundary as a lane on the motorway. The clearer they are, the easier it is for people to drive. The same goes when it comes to unconditional love, it can flow like a rainbow from one side to the other.

"To love unconditionally requires no contracts, bargains, or agreements. Love exists in the moment-to-moment flux of life." (Marion Woodman)

CHAPTER 3

FAITH, BELIEF, AND WILL POWER

"A life without believing is like a life without music."

Faith and belief mean the same thing. Some people prefer to use the notion of belief, while others are drawn to the one of faith. No matter which notion you prefer, it all comes back to trusting something or someone completely. This is a subconscious program created in our minds, ever since we were little, due to our life experiences at the time. For instance, your dad told you repeatedly, as a little kid, that you can achieve anything you want and that you are fearless. Well, that was embedded in your mind. As a teenager or adult, you will have high self-esteem and self-worth. You will not be shy when it comes to acting. Or maybe it was the other way around and your dad continuously beat you, stating that you're no good and he wishes that you were never born. As a kid, such actions and words have a powerful effect, leading to a very low self-esteem, with all sorts of fears and traumas carried into teenage and adulthood.

Beliefs are mostly created under the age of six, when our brain is like a sponge, and it absorbs everything with ease. So whatever we have been told or saw happening around us, from parents, teachers, or other family members, especially the older ones, we perceived as real. As a result, we have developed a belief system that made us who we are and influences our actions in the present. If your parents were smokers, there is a huge chance that you will be a smoker too. You will carry a heavier emotional package, as people smoke because they are suppressing certain emotions.

As a kid, you may have noticed that your parents were smoking because they did not have enough money but never had the courage to admit it. Instead, they were lying to themselves that it was all good. Well, guess what? Growing up, you would have already unconsciously picked that emotional baggage. As a result, you will smoke when certain issues in your life appear, as you are choosing to suppress rather than accept your emotions. You might shy away from acknowledging your problems, choosing not to deal with them.

If you are the responsible kind, then do not to let it take you down and keep you there. Love yourself, even though that problem obviously leads to hurt or makes you feel uncomfortable. Because, let's be honest, life will bring many issues and problems, because that's how it is. That doesn't mean that we must run away and hide behind drugs, alcohol, or any other harmful coping strategy, running away from reality. Instead, we must understand that life has defining moments. You are tried, and if you can pass the test, you will grow. These life lessons can help us evolve.

There is another thing that can help us, whenever a problem arises. I am talking about being able to change your perception. So, if you have been kicked out from your job, try to understand that it all happens for a reason. You are going to find a better job, where you will be better paid, or maybe discover a business opportunity that you wouldn't have come across if you were still at that job, one which requires more of your attention. Even if you don't have any money, don't worry that much, instead focus on how you can make more somewhere else.

Marcus Aurelius, my mentor, used to say that one should transform any obstacle that's in his/her way into material. By changing your perception about what happened, looking at the full half of your glass, you will benefit from a better outcome. Thus, you have something to work with. If you had given up already, well, there isn't much to do, is there? The change in perception will improve your life significantly. If you have dreams, and I know that everybody has, here is how to talk to yourself. "I will make it, no matter what, and nothing can stop me. Even though I will encounter obstacles, I will never give up, because I have the right to succeed". Repeat these words until you believe them, and I promise you that you will make it.

I remember reading so many books on personal development. After a while, whatever came my way, I knew that I could achieve it, both subconsciously and consciously. I wasn't scared or afraid, and I would embrace any problem or obstacle knowing that was my moment of growth. I was grateful and thankful to the universe for that. My friends would come to me and asked how much money I wanted to make, and I would say ten million. Looking back, I understand that I was limiting myself by saying that. They would laugh and look at me with doubt, asking how I was going to achieve that. And I would reply to them, I don't know, but the answer lies within me, and I deserve it.

For as long as, I had air in my lungs, I would find ways to make that happen, because it was part of my dream and I wanted it so bad that nothing could stay in my way. I would go through anything, and if I couldn't go through, I would go around or above, because there are always ways to succeed, you only need to really want it. So do not ever let anyone tell you different. Their beliefs, along with their fears and limitations, do not belong to you. Only you can set you the bar as high as you want. Just because they don't know how to achieve it, that doesn't mean that the rest should follow. Besides, what do they really know about your dream? They don't carry that fire in their belly like you do. So never let anyone tell you otherwise. You owe it to yourself to take charge and responsibility, and let your dreams unfold.

When I was sleeping in the park, next to a big rock, so that I was a bit protected by wind, if somebody were to tell me then, don't worry one, day you will grow up and build your own house, with your own two hands and your money, I would have not believed that. I was too little and too scared to be able to tap into that belief.

I will keep saying both words in this chapter, belief, and faith, as I don't want to upset anybody, because of my choice. How do we tap into faith, or what does it mean for us? It might bear a slightly different meaning for each person, as some people believe that faith has to do with religion or spirituality, which is true to an extent. Otherwise, if you only have faith in your religion, considering it to be the best, with your God as the only one to exist, that is extreme thinking. This can be limiting, and it belongs to the group of people who refuse to accept the other people inhabiting this planet, perceiving them as outsiders, who are always in the wrong.

Let's be honest, that's not God's wish. I don't think that Buddha, Allah. the Christian God, or any other source of high energy, says that it only loves a few and the rest can just die in all sorts of hells.

This is a political and spiritual talk, and I'm not going to debate this topic in this book, I will save it for another time. To understand faith, we must have beliefs. This is of monumental importance in every human's life. Without it, life will just be harder. Imagine a life without music, that's how a life without beliefs would be. Not only do they keep us afloat when we don't understand life, but they help us when we are in despair and traumatic experiences take over our life. For instance, when you become homeless, when a parent dies, or even worse when a child dies before his/her parents.

In such cases, modern medicine doesn't do squat, it might only numb the pain we experience. Believe it or not, this is a very clever strategy. Every year, millions of people take various medications, searching for healing. The truth is that only the belief in a higher self or spirituality can aid and heal over time. I am not trying to denigrate western medicine, which has its own benefits and is very advanced nowadays. It represents the only solution when it comes to organ transplants and replacing other parts in the human body. If you cut your fingers with a circular saw, you will not go into a deep prayer with your God, so that your fingers grow back. You will call the emergency service and talk to God later.

When you have lived a traumatic experience, there is a historical fact, which has been cautiously erased from our books. I am talking about having faith in a divine source of energy. It is always there for us to listen, relieve our pains and sorrows. We can access through our prayers and meditations. There is nothing better than the pain released from a burdened heart, that feeling of lightness derived from faith makes. With patience, it can lead to miracles every time. And not only that, but thanks to it, we can tap into something else, which will offer a better understanding of how to live and let live.

I'll give you an example. I was preparing myself for a meditation session the other day, and so I lit a few candles and put my pillows on the floor. My left shoulder had been in deep pain for almost a month, ever since I fell on it during a yoga pose. I went to massage therapy several times and did some exercises, but the pain was still there, and the therapist kept telling me that I was okay and that she can't find anything to be wrong with my shoulder. Regardless, the pain was there and whilst I was meditating, I went on a little spiritual journey to find out more about the pain. And my God, I discovered more than I was expecting.

I first asked what was happening with my shoulder. A higher voice told me that the problem is not the muscle strain, but rather an old belief that decided to sit down for a cup of tea, like my wife likes to call it. Let me tell you how it all started and what happened. I had a limiting belief, thinking that if I wore my wedding ring whilst I did my workout, I would feel uncomfortable and I would eventually hurt myself. This happened. As I practiced my handstand, I interlocked my fingers behind the back of my head. I put too much pressure on my fingers and lost my balance, therefore falling backwards on my left shoulder. That was not all, just the starting point.

A few days later, prior to my meditation, I had a fight with my wife. That was followed by a series of events, just like Murphy's laws, which led me to tap into my old belief that I was superior to everyone else, and I became rigid in my thinking, with a similar effect over my emotions. Therefore, I couldn't let go, even though I knew that I was punishing myself more than anybody else by being rigid. So, after I realized that I was blaming my ring for the accident, instead of taking responsibility, I then let go of that limiting belief and my pain was instantly released. As soon as I finished my meditation, I noticed that the pain was gone, and it felt good. Just like I previously stated, there is nothing better than a light heart or an inner pain that has been lifted.

I know what some might think, especially those who put their faith in science. You might say that it was nothing, but placebo, an illusion, and the pain will return at some point. I am not here to argue with what you or others believe in, I just want to point out that what you believe in manifests one way or the other. Whether you want to acknowledge it or not, it will manifest. If you believe in science, remember that if you can manage to combine the two, life on Earth becomes lighter, more vibrant, and full of amazing new discoveries to unfold.

Let me tell you about an incredible scientific discovery. An experiment was conducted in the winter of 2001, in Sri Lanka, where almost two hundred thousand people meditated for peace, against the background of war. Shortly after that, spiritual masters managed to gather over half a million of people together, to meditate for peace and love, a kindness-based meditation. The attacks taking place throughout the country stopped, the firing ceased, and the governments eventually came to an agreement. You can find more about this online.

What I am trying to say and prove is that when science and spirituality merge together, miracles can happen. Imagine how you would like to manifest the purchase of a new car. You envision it and maybe go to the dealership to get into the car. Then, you write it down and meditate on it. This usually works if done properly, from the energy of one single human. Now, imagine five hundred thousand people put together, all their energy focused on one purpose only, peace, which was absolutely incredible.

In the field of quantum physics, they say that things change accordingly to how you look at them. Let me offer an example, so that you can understand the negative and positive perspectives. Imagine that you see a little puppy on the street, who is hurt, because he ate some rat poison. He is in pain and shaking, and maybe he is even bleeding. If you go towards the puppy with a lot of negative energy, thinking that he is going to die or being afraid of that outcome, and you don't know what to do or how to react and treat him, you will have a strong magnetic pull. That will enter the puppy's vortex of energy and he will feel it, which in turn will affect him significantly.

Now imagine the opposite. You are going towards the puppy, with compassion and love in your heart. As a result, your brain creates new pathways, never seen before. It will create ideas, so that you are able to deal with the situation. Maybe you will give him some water with salt, so that he can vomit the swallowed poison. You might offer him shelter and take him to a veterinarian. By having this mindset, your whole energy shifts, alongside with the puppy, which now has a chance to live.

Remember that we have a strong life-giving energy, capable of creation, which lies dormant within us. Once our channels of energy are open, it is very easy for it to flow through us, and it can help us or others heal.

Willpower, on the other hand, is something that we build through our experiences and conditioning. We can be change how we feel, as willpower is rather connected to our solar plexus, where strong doing emotions lie. That's why the expression "to have guts" resonates with having willpower, because to achieve things, one must "have the guts" to do what he/she wants.

How do we tap into willpower? And how we maintain it? That's something that we are all interested in. Well, to find out what we love doing, we must try new things all the time and fail repeatedly, until our business is in alignment with our mind, body, and spirit. To get there, we must do many uncomfortable things, such as learning a new skill, a new sport, or workout, which sometimes can become frustrating. By trying new things our "willingness" builds up, like a muscle that is worked out all the time.

Let's say you have been working on a new business, and two or five years later it doesn't resonate with you anymore, or it's simply not working for your purpose. It will be hard to drop all that energy and time, which you have invested into learning new skills, so as to improve yourself. But if you look at the full half of the glass, you will realize that you have learned some skills. These can be added to your personal resume, not just to the professional one. Over time, they might prove to be useful, for you and others. It is not wasted time as some might think, because everything in life happens for a reason.

So, every time you try a new job, new skill, new workout, and so on, it will add up to your willpower and never-giving-up attitude. The secret is to keep going and push forward, to be your greatest version in this lifetime. Another secret regards delayed gratification, something only few people are privileged to achieve. They are willing to work on it and to maintain it, no matter what life brings their way, whether is good or bad. You must also find the will to stay alive and evolve as a respectful human being, someone who can move through life, no matter what happens along the way. If you have that ability to control yourself, with strong determination, then you will be able to move mountains.

To act from that perspective, one mustn't give into the role of victim in life but work to reverse it. Whatever hardship you encounter, use it as fuel to upgrade yourself, and look at it as a learning curve. Once you have managed to tap into your willpower, you will have great benefits to gain. Imagine that you can delay gratification and resist short term temptations. That alone will put you in the control of your life, so that you can take charge.

Imagine a person who wants an expensive car, just to show off around the neighbourhood, to his girlfriend or friends. Because they have no patience or self-control, they will start making massive mistakes that will lead to their downfall. They might take big loans from the bank or their family, getting kicked out from their job. Then, a recession comes and the downwards spiral will start. They might not have enough money to repay their loan, having to sell stuff around the house, just to keep a lifestyle that nobody cares of, but their inflated ego.

Over time, the car will lose its value, and they will not be able to sell it for the same amount, not even half of the buying price. They will end up selling it anyway, just to pay a part of the loan back. In consequence, they will have no car, no money, and low self-esteem. Their new situation will lead to anxiety, and maybe drinking problems, all just because they had no self-control.

Things would have stood differently if they had self-control and willpower. There is nothing wrong with wishing to buy an expensive car, but one must assess the situation very well and understand that sometimes it is better to wait for a couple of years. It is for the best to work towards financial independence, and then maybe one can afford to buy whatever they desire. Delayed gratification can help one go a long way, with cleverer decisions being taken, decisions that are not based on a weak mind and a frail ego.

Another example would involve sweets, such as cookies. I bet that millions of people resonate with this one. If you eat a chocolate as soon as your mind has asked for it, that is a sign of weakness. Let's say that you are on the road driving and get hungry, craving something sweet. If you wait until you get home to have a cooked meal or something healthier, before that chocolate, that my friend right there is proof of character. Not only will your body thank you, but once it's becoming a habit, you will also increase your willpower and self-control. It might take some time, but you'll get there if that is what you wish. With time and practice, anything can be achieved.

Remember that we are habitual beings, which means that we don't really abandon a habit. We rather change it for another and let us just hope that it is a better one. I used to be an addict of all sorts, with sugar being one of my weaknesses. Trust me when I say that it took me years and years to try and change that habit of eating processed sugar and sweets, which were usually placed at the entrance or exit of every shop in this world.

I think that we all know by now why all those sweets with colourful wrappers are placed there. When you enter the shop, you will buy at least one or if not, you will get it on your way out, after you finish your shopping, nice and easy. Those bright colours are affecting children the most, because to child colours mean happiness. And not to stop there, but once I understood the negative effect of sweets, I thought that was it. I will stop eating sugar, which didn't really help long term because the human body requires a certain amount of sugar.

After I watched several documentaries on sugar, I found out how to change my habit. Basically, I had to start eating more fruits that contained sugar, therefore keeping my sugar level up, but in a healthy manner. And this is how I've changed one habit with another, and you could do the same with anything. If you smoke, try and find something healthier instead, and I don't mean replacing tobacco with weed, that's not going to help. Try a few exercises instead, some push-ups or squats every day, it is all about finding a healthy balance and increasing that willpower, until you can move mountains.

By the end of this book, if you apply at least half of what I suggested, you will be amazed to discover that you can increase your self-worth and willpower by at least three hundred percent. Remember that believing is healthy, and sometimes it can help more than western medicine. Whether it's God or a goal that you put your faith in, do it one hundred percent, with no remorse. Even if you fail, you would have learned something. Your willpower will increase through different experiences. Trying new things and even failing will help you understand that it wasn't all in vain if you look at the full half of the glass.

CHAPTER 4

EDUCATION

"The only person you are destined to become is the person you decide to be."
(Ralph Waldo Emerson)

What is education? And why is a specific agenda pushed so much by governments? Do we really need it the way it's being portrayed? Let us dive into it.

I did not excel in school, and this might have something to do with the fact that I was neurodivergent. I haven't finished masters or doctorates of any sorts because nothing that I was taught in school drew my interest. From my point of view, not only is the educational system limited but it also acts as a heavy brain-washing machine, affecting the future generations on this planet. First, through school, you can become only what they teach you, doctor, carpenter, engineer, musician, and a few other options. But these options are made in such a clever, yet nasty way, so that you grow up with the idea of being able to make it in life only through a few options.

Imagine being a millionaire and a free person, working as a car mechanic. It is not impossible, but if you look at the data, only 1% make it. Tell me how many of the remaining 99% out there like being smeared with grease and dirt all day, just to make a lousy wage, having to raise a family, pay for a house, and cover all the living costs, for the rest of their lives. Don't get me wrong, I understand, and I respect the fact that there are people out there who like being a mechanic or a decorator. Yet, no matter how much they love it, even they think it is not worth it, given the wages that are offered on the market, especially in third world countries.

The exception would be when they have a side hustle. This will help them make more money. Otherwise, they are trapped in a rat race, just like the other 80% of the population. Trust me, I know, because I've been stuck in the exact same situation for decades. It is not, nor will it ever be a shame to do a physical job, one in which hard labour is involved, if you take care of yourself and pay your bills to the government, and to the ones who are already rich. What I find shameful is the level of payment the working-class benefits from.

That's why education is important. However, I am not talking about the old ways, the methods that they have used to teach past generations. Education should unfold with more creativity and passion, not with that old school strictness, where if you don't know the answers to various questions, you will be graded accordingly, and they will attack your self-esteem. I graduated from college in Romania when I was eighteen years old. This means they had ten years to shape and brainwash the next future carpenter, because that's what society needed, another carpenter who belongs to the working class, someone to build nice houses for the rich.

I didn't like being a carpenter, but due to my grades at the time, that was one of my few options. I had to become a working-class man. If I wouldn't do that, I would've had my future threatened. I would have been without a job, unable to have a house and lacking the needed freedom. And I know that I have free will, but think about it. I was eighteen years old, immature, and brain washed. Just a kid. Did I really have a choice? Maybe yes, maybe no. One thing is certain. As soon as I had my passport, I left Eastern Europe, bound for the western part of the continent, where I made money and created my own future.

Even though I had been brainwashed for ten years, I still acted on my free will. With a little bit of help from some friends, I gravitated towards the big, wide capitalist western world. Let me tell you how much my so-promised carpenter diploma has helped me in life, from zero to none. I have been lied a gazillion times before, so this wasn't news to me. Nobody told me that if you finish school, they will ask you for experience before getting a job. Nevertheless, I accepted all sorts of jobs along the years, and nobody asked me about my diploma. In construction all they cared about was to be young and healthy, so that they could work you to the max as a labourer for a lousy pay.

I'm not saying that you can't make money and be free by studying to become a doctor or a lawyer, but the chances for you to achieve that are 15%. Most people do their jobs, just because they have been pushed by their parents and because they must pay the bills. Only few love their job and make enough money to also buy their freedom. If you are one of them, consider yourself lucky and enjoy life because not everybody can.

The worst thing about school is that they don't teach kids, the future generations, how to make money or how to be creative, and I'm not referring only to music, painting, or sculpting. The human mind is immensely creative, and the school curriculum should encourage the pursuit of creativity. It should also focus on the human body and its health. Children should be taught how to become great speakers, as this is a great asset. They should learn how to make money, and how to become emotionally and financially free. That is a necessity for all the humans of this planet, we do not need more carpenters and house painters. Instead, we need to teach children how to behave, with education helping them develop a positive mindset and great virtues, as all these things are essential.

I am not trying to attack all the educational systems in Europe, because apparently there are some countries that are being praised for their educational efforts, such as Finland, the United Kingdom, the Netherlands, or Sweden. My moment of clarity came at the age of twenty-four, when I realized how much I lacked in terms of education. I understood that I had to evolve and educate myself, so that I could become what I wanted in this lifetime. And so, I picked up a book, then two, then three, until I was reading about two to three books a week. Reading helped me in different areas of my life. The more I read, the more I loved it.

I started focusing on personal development books, because that is the topic, I am most passionate about. I understood that education is meant to be an enlightened experience, helping you learn how to work for yourself and not for others, or along other people, as a team with mutual benefits.

I will say this. If you are passionate about one thing, deeply and truthfully, then buy all the books and courses on that topic. Go to seminars, wake up with it in your mind, and go to sleep thinking about the same thing. It might not help you make money in the beginning, but trust me, money will follow over time. You might not have enough, but this blockage will be released through the love you dedicate to your passion.

Imagine trying to become a painter, wanting the money and the benefits that come with it. First, you must be talented. If you don't have talent, don't worry, discipline beats talent any time of the day. You must read everything about the great ones, like da Vinci, Monet, or Picasso, or any other new and modern artist. Buy courses on how to paint, gain the necessary skills and knowledge, and experience will come with your growth. Money will follow and freedom will come, but don't expect instant gratification.

Let me tell you a little story that some of you might have heard before. Leonardo da Vinci, one of the greatest renaissance painters and scientists, was in a market one day, painting. A lady passed by, asking him if he can do her portrait in exchange for money. He accepted, and five minutes later he handed over her portrait, asking for a large sum of money. The lady was puzzled, inquiring why he asked for so much. She said it was unbelievable, as he had only worked for five minutes and wanted so much money. The artist replied to the young lady that it had taken him over thirty years of hard work and practice, to be able to learn to do this in five minutes. This story teaches us about self-worth, and how to respect yourself after all the hard work that you have been doing, refusing to sell your time for cheap.

If you are patient and stay disciplined, such habits will set you free. Look at some of the richest people in the world, people who haven't even been to college. They made it big and became great, making important sums of money. People like Steve Jobs, the guy who created Apple, Bill Gates, the founder of Microsoft, Richard Branson, who dropped out of school at the age of sixteen and now owns Virgin, Roman Abramovich, who used to sell plastic toys out of his apartment in Russia and now is worth thirteen billion dollars. The list is impressive, and I could go on and on, but I assume that you get the point.

You don't have to have a degree to become rich, but you do need to educate yourself. Being lucky is not enough, this only applies to a limited number of people. And, usually due to the lack of discipline, you won't end up very balanced. By adding personal development education to your lifestyle, this will improve your emotional intelligence and the ability to manage your own emotions, as well as the ones of others. This is critical to building and maintaining relationships.

It is not something that you can learn from a young age in public school, where if you've made a mistake, you must endure shame, guilt, or punishment, instead of learning the necessary coping mechanisms, which will help you handle conflicts and challenges. As kids, we made mistakes every day. We were "educated" by impatient teachers, people who had their own unresolved problems at home, which will bring to class. They had no patience, with all their problems, traumas, and insecurities influencing a room full of kids, tiny humans who were like a sponge at that young age.

Some kids are troublemakers and have no filter. I am not saying that it's the teacher's fault, because there are many teachers out there who truly love kids and that is why they chose this career path. Maybe at home they received the same amount of education from an emotional point of view, from their parents and other elders around their household. It is just the way the system is built, which is not appropriate for the growth and healthy evolution of our kids.

Imagine if personal development would be taught at a young age. This would help individuals develop a sense of meaning and purpose in their lives. By exploring their values, interests, and passions, they can identify what is important for them and what they want to become in life, with a positive sense of free will. In turn, this will most likely turn lost and misunderstood young kids into healthy, creative, and balanced human beings who can achieve meaningful goals. They will make this world a better place, united and not divided, so that power is present.

I know this isn't going to happen any time soon. Until then, I would like to introduce you to a powerful method, named after the ancient Greek philosopher Socrates, known as the "Socratic questioning". This ten-question structure can help you develop greater emotional intelligence, as you will challenge your own assumptions and beliefs, becoming more open-minded and receptive to new ideas and perspectives. Many CBT practitioners and therapists use this technique to help others in their life as well as themselves. It involves a series of questions that are designed to help you explore your own thinking and assumptions. These are open-ended, focusing on the underlying reasoning and assumptions behind a particular belief system. If you ever feel stuck or have a negative thinking pattern, just go through the questionnaire.

Thought or belief to be questioned.

Example: I believe that I am a bad parent

1 What is the evidence that you have for this thought?

2 What is the evidence against it?

3 Is this thought based on facts or feelings?

4 Is this thought black and white, or more complex?

5 Is there any chance that you might misinterpret the evidence?

6 Are you making any assumptions?

7 Might other people have a different interpretation of this situation? What is it?

8 Are you looking at all the evidence or just the one that supports your thought?

9 Could your thoughts be an exaggeration of what is true?

10 Are you having this thought out of habit or do the facts support it?

11 Could there be someone who passed this thought onto you?

12 If so, is it a reliable source?

13 Is that thought a likely scenario or a worst-case scenario?

14 If worst is black and likely is white, how much space is there between them?

     These questions are designed to help you clarify your thinking, to discover what evidence you have that support your claim, and to challenge the underlying assumptions or beliefs behind a statement or argument. As a result, you will understand if there is evidence to support a particular assumption. You will explore the consequences of a particular belief or action, by examining the alternatives of what would happen, if you were to consider a different approach. This type of questioning is used in counselling, education, and coaching, representing a powerful tool for personal development and a more balanced mind.

     Finally, your education will determine your success in life, whatever that might be. I understand that for some people education might be a close synonym to discipline. However, if you truly understand the true benefits of an authentic human education, you can become the happiest man or woman alive. I am talking about the education that you should apply to your personal life, business, and career, as well as passion. If you want to become the next Picasso, start reading all the books available on painting and art in general, take courses or watch videos on how to become a painter, for the next five or ten years of your life. What do you think is the worst that can happen?

     Expanding your knowledge might scare you. Do it anyway, because the happiness and fulfilment in this lifetime of yours will depend on it. What would you rather choose? To try and learn new things for the next five years, whether it will take you out of your comfort zone and make you feel uncomfortable, and maybe cause you to lose a few friends or relationships, as following your dreams can become a lonely road, or would you rather live led by another's person dream and maybe work for them, to accomplish their dreams for the rest of your life? Nobody says that it is easy. Those who are saying this, they are lying, however, you should make bravery one of your virtues of life.

     It takes courage to leave things and people behind, it takes courage to put yourself out there, to attend seminars or courses, to engage with new people, and build new and healthier relationships, especially if you have an introverted personality, or carry any other traumatic experiences from the past that block you from being able to meet new people, or talk in public, or any other traumatic experiences that led to low self-esteem. Make this one more reason to dive into the self-help education, and allow it to guide you, and help you move further up in life. I want to end this chapter with one of the greatest philosophers, who used to roam this Earth and share his wisdom over two thousand years ago.

"Education is the kindling of the flame, not the filling of the vessel." (Socrates)

CHAPTER 5
DISCIPLINE

"Discipline over desires". (Marcus Aurelius)

The Oxford dictionary defines the word *discipline* as, 'the practice of training people to obey rules or a code of behaviour, using punishments to correct disobedience." I think it sounds a bit rough and has a bad connotation for everybody. I perceive discipline differently. In my opinion, if you apply it in every area of your life, you can achieve anything you want. A wise person once said that the magic of discipline is that it can make anything possible. To introduce discipline in your life, so that you can be in control of your life and habits, there are some things you must apply.

Number 1 Know your strengths and weaknesses.

"Your weaknesses represent the reversed reflection of your biggest power."

Creating your pillars as a foundation:

When you know what you're good at, it will be much easier to act on your goals with confidence. Your self-esteem and self-worth will increase exponentially, leading you to a clear and focused path. Let me give you an example. I'm good at working out. Not only that I'm good at training, but I do it every day with enjoyment, and that is one of my pillars for my health, wealth, and personal development in life.

What do I mean when I say pillars? I refer to something that I set my mind and body to do daily, even if I don't feel like doing it, even if something bad is happening from an emotional point of view, if I get kicked out of my job, my team, my family, or if I lose something valuable like money or relationships. Unless something is wrong with my health, I won't stop. Having a pillar like that in life is very important when things go wrong, and I can't rely on someone else. I've got my work out as a base, which will give me more than if I had chosen not to do it.

Here is an example. I will make it a bit extreme, but sometimes life is like that. It can be unfair and there is nothing we can do about it. Let's say that my dad has died. I have the option to mourn him and probably start drinking, and maybe become another heavy load, instead of supporting my family. Or I can mourn him, which is natural, but at the same time do my workout. This would help me stay healthy from a physical point of view, as well as focused on a mental level.

I would be able to prepare the funeral, to lift his dead body, and not drop it on the floor because I'm too drunk. I would choose to wake up early, and benefit from the balance and support that a workout guaranteed. As a result, I could support my family and bury my dad as expected. The alternative would be to fall into a trap set by my own mind. My dad died and I would choose to bury my sorrows, as well as all the old good or bad memories I have of him, drinking for the next few months. I would slip into a negative behaviour, and I doubt that my father would want me to do such things, once he would no longer be part of this world.

There are many African, even Mexican cultures, which celebrate the dead, as they have understood they are in a better place. When somebody dies, that should be a time for celebration, not crying and mourning. Living in the western society, we suffer when we lose someone. Most religions believe the dead are gone forever, never to be seen again. The human ego is very frail, and we get easily attached to the notion of having a physical body. But if you understand that unconditional love means letting go of such attachments, you will be free of suffering.

Maybe my example was a bit extreme, but I think you get the picture. Emotional imbalance can very easily cause you to drift away from your life's purpose if you don't create your own pillars. So, with that being said. Creating your pillars is like the foundation of your house. You want it to be made of stone, concrete, or metal, so that when an earthquake happens it stands still, maybe it will move a bit from left to right, but it won't fall.

Think about it. The more pillars you will have built, the easier the life becomes. That should be one of your purposes in life. Don't suffer in pain and live a life of quiet desperation. And if you are in pain, dealing with suffering, at least choose to change. Fight to improve your life, as it is your birth right, and keep on working hard. Push until you will be able to see the light on the end of your tunnel. Create your own destiny and don't give the power that is yours to other people who do not deserve it or think they can take your energy away, like a vampire in the night. You can do what other people can't even dream of, because you're special and you deserve it.

Find and explore your weaknesses to know where to improve:

When you acknowledge your weaknesses, you know where improvements are necessary. You can work on yourself and upgrade your skills. Remember, we must have the courage to ask for help whenever we need it, even if most of the times our ego won't let us. I respect that you want to make it by yourself and be independent, which is very good, but it is essential to understand that even the best of the best people need help at times. Let's face the mirror often, as we are not always operating from our highest level. My biggest weaknesses in life were the unhealthy attachment and the lack of justice. It all started with my childhood trauma when my mum abandoned me at the age of four and my dad dropped me in a different city to his parents' house.

There have been many moments in my life when I've been through many breakups, in different relationships. Because I've attached myself too much to those people, when we broke up, I felt bad for months. I wasn't capable to detach myself emotionally and take control of my life. I let myself to be controlled by emotions, which eventually led me to significant procrastination. I started to smoke again, even though I had quit for months or even years, and I started drinking like an alcoholic every day. I stopped going to the gym and abandoned all my personal development programs, which were going great at the time, and I replaced everything with laziness, being irresponsible.

I planned on abandoning work as well. I've spent ample amounts of money over the course of several months, on things I didn't need, as well as on alcohol. I was hurting myself and everyone around me. A major shift took place in my life at the time, in the worst way possible, related to my last breakup. Until one day, when I decided to call my best friend, with whom I hadn't spoken for about a year. I've been through a period where I wanted to be alone, away from the world, such as family and friends, so I could find myself.

I was explaining the situation to my best friend. We met several times to talk. One day he told me that what I was doing was not healthy, and that I should take care of myself and take my life back. Even though he doesn't know, I am deeply grateful to him, because he has helped me overcome a difficult moment in my life. When we don't have the mental or emotional capacity to maintain life in a vital balance, it is essential to listen to the people who care for us. Emi, if you're reading this book, I am deeply grateful to you, and I thank you from the bottom of my heart.

You ask why I didn't encourage myself. Maybe I could have patted my own back, utter several motivational phrases, dust myself off, and move on with my life. It's easy to say such things, as opposed to taking action. Sometimes, a dark veil of cloudiness surrounds our head, our mind is filled with negative thoughts, and our body is filled with toxins, like alcohol and cigarettes. You need a different kind of energy to shift your perceptions, like the one of a friend, as it was in my case. Do not get fooled, the devil is alive, and its ways and shapes are as you give them life to become. Only you can bring it to life, no one else. At the same time, you hold the power to slay it and operate from your higher self.

At the time, I didn't know that the desire for attachment was my weakness. I did not realize how it could hurt me. Shortly after the few chats with my friend, a couple of introspections, a lot of money lost, and some emotional damage, I realised where I needed to heal and improve myself. How did I do that? Simple. I started to practise self-love and taking care of my mind, body, and spirit. I've started meditating again, so I could have my mental and spiritual balance back. I started working out, to cleanse and detoxify my body of all those months of alcohol and other cheap drugs. And so, I brought harmony back into my life.

The biggest lesson is to understand that our biggest fears, or what we perceive as weaknesses, represent in fact the reversed reflection of our biggest power. Once you learn how to use it to your advantage, as it happened in my case, your life will be amazing. I learned from abandonment; it became my path towards learning. I discovered what unconditional love was, by letting go of the suffering that my ego has attached to my mind.

As humans, it is our duty to fight against all odds sometimes. Life is unfair and unjust; we notice this often around the world. Greed takes over one's mind, with the respective person wanting to conquer everything. Innocent people from different countries, including children, are killed, as others want to take their resources. Nations are suppressed, with people like this clearly proving that they are uncontrollable and imbalanced.

It is impressive to discover that somebody from a third-world country, with no means of making it out alive, with a low chance of progress in life, has managed to become one of the greatest people of his era. Elie Wiesel received the Novel prize for peace. He was born in Romania in 1928 and he was one of the Holocaust survivors, having been captured and kept as prisoner at Auschwitz, in 1944. Up to that dreadful turn, he was living in the northern part of Romania, in Sighetu Marmatiei and he was only fifteen years old.

He was freed by the Allied Forces in 1945, but most of his family had died, his mother, a younger sister, and his father. After the war, he went to Sorbonne, in France, where he studied journalism. This helped him to publish his book, a memoir of his experience in the concentration camps. He then moved to the United States, continuing to fight for the human rights. He became a professor at Boston university, his life journey coming to an end in 2016. The university created the "Elie Wiesel Centre for Jewish Studies" in his honour, as recognition for his contribution to Jewish causes and the fight for human rights.

Victor Frankl was a psychiatrist, who survived the Holocaust with a completely different perception. You can check out one of his many books, "Man's Search for Meaning", to understand the power of one's mind, even when it is put through hell. Mike Tyson had a tough childhood, but he became the best and was eventually inducted into the Boxing Hall of Fame. He turned his weakness and pain into greatness. He is a wise and inspiring person now.

The list can go on and on. Be careful not to fall into the trap where you think that all heroes wear a cape and are what they are advertised to be. Please do your research, as you don't want to become one of those billionaires who made it grand on the backs of the little children from third-world countries. Indeed, it often happens that we fail to see what is really happening, because of the fake media reports.

Eliminate distractions and temptations from your goals:

"Alchemy is an inner superpower that we can tap into once we have a clear mind and a clean body."

It is very important to understand that we are like the people that we spend our time with, and those surround us. If we have friends who make £20.000 per year, we will gain the same. But if we surround ourselves with people who make £100.000 per year, guess what… Exactly! We will make about the same amount of money. This goes for everything in our lives, not just finances, but also when it comes to emotional health, relationships, etc. This is essential to acknowledge, especially if procrastination is a frequent habit.

If your friends have drinking problems or are addicted to drugs, including cocaine, prescription pills, marijuana, heroin, or other synthetic drugs, I think it is clear where they will end up. This is called the master mind effect, and it can work in both directions, meaning positive and negative. It depends on how one will apply it. Please choose your friends wisely. If anyone in your life has a negative influence over you, distance yourself. Even if they are part of the family, it doesn't matter. I'm not asking you to give into hate, but to separate yourself from them. Explain to them that you are following your dream, and how their toxic ways affect your journey, keeping you back.

The tantric practice, which is a spiritual practice towards enlightenment, has much to teach us. The core of this practice refers to the following. When you come across pleasure, one should not ignore or supress it, but to accept and release or let go of it, so that one is truly free. For example, if you feel attracted to a person of another sex, do not let yourself be controlled by those emotions, which will undoubtedly make you do extraordinary things at times. Control yourself and understand the urge you have towards that person or whatever it might be, that urge is distorting your perception. In short, it will make a mountain out of a molehill.

This applies to any distraction out there, like eating unhealthy foods, drinking, smoking, gambling, bad relationships, and so on. All of these are temporary, they last only for a short period of time, and are not fulfilling, nor will they bring you true happiness or joy. That is why you must practice some sort of alchemy, which will help you redirect your energy from bad habits. You will then focus on achieving your goals and dreams, which in time will bring you true happiness and fulfilment.

By practicing alchemy, you will strengthen your focus and become a more cerebral human being. Alchemy is an inner superpower; this is how I like to perceive it. Through your mentality and willpower, you will be able to change bad habits into healthy ones, just by choosing to do so. Like alchemists used to change metal into gold, this is I like to interpret this metaphor. We will discuss about that later in the book.

Here is an example of a bad pattern.

Seven years in a row, despite having discovered personal development, I followed a destructive pattern, one which I am going to share with you. I had started my personal development journey, and by that, I mean that I was following my dream every day, through a set of practices, such as physical, mental, and spiritual. In the first year, I kept abandoning my program every two to three months. There were barriers or resistances in my way, and I couldn't follow through, because I kept letting myself get distracted by friends, who wanted to go to the pub or to a club. I was falling for it every time, and the same thing happened. There were two to three months in which I worked on myself, after which I would destroy all that, I had been building.

In the second year, I started strong, thinking that I had learned from last year's mistakes. All was going nice and well, until I got into a relationship, which made me lose my focus. I forgot my goals for about a year, and we eventually broke up. I am not saying that if you want to go through personal development, you must break up, divorce, or anything like that, God no. However, if you're in a relationship this journey might be more difficult because the person next to you needs attention, something normal in any relationship.

I realized that I couldn't find the needed balance while in a relationship, it seemed impossible to work on my dreams. I remembered the quote, "If you want to go fast go alone, but if you want to go far go together". And I wanted to go fast. I started the third year in force. I visited the gym on a regular basis, read two hours each day, played the violin, learned a new language. I got into college, started my own business, printing T-shirts. I had extraordinary plans, firmly convinced that year was going to be amazing.

One day, while I was in college, this new girl showed up. She had wonderful hair and nice hips, and I fell for her, just like a teenager. I ended up in a new relationship and all my attention was focused on her. Thus, I lost myself and everything that I had built up to that point. I started drinking, smoking, and doing drugs again, as a non-stop leisure, losing my interest in personal development and self-love. It was as if I didn't learn the lessons from the previous years. I know, I know, but this is what happens with us humans, when we don't have control over our emotions. We are prone to making the same mistake repeatedly, until we realise that it's not good.

I managed to break through this unhealthy pattern. And I've understood that if I want to help people to grow, I must be able to help myself first, and I don't mean that in a selfish way. Because I have realised that when I feel fantastic, everyone around me feels the same. That's because I have chosen to work on myself intensely, for a period of two to three years, or as many as necessary to achieve my goals. I want to build up a strong, never-give-up kind of character, and a strong personality, so that I cannot be distracted from my goals ever again. Thus, I will be able to create a life that I don't need a holiday from, and then I will be able to redirect my energy towards a healthy and nourishing relationship. Until then, I promise to lose not even one minute. Like Bruce Lee said, "If you love life, don't lose time, because that's what life is made of".

Set your goals and implement them:

"Success takes place when dreams are bigger that excuses." (Unknown)

When it comes to goals, it is essential to have a pen and paper on which to write them down. Research shows that those who write down their goals are nearly twice as likely to accomplish them, as writing sends a direct message to the brain. And it is very important not to limit yourself on what you want to achieve, if it's not absurd, such as wanting to make a billion Euros in a week or becoming a dolphin. I don't know what you would like to achieve, but I suggest that you engage in this mental practice for at least a week or even more, until you get it.

Find a quiet place, go into nature, or wherever you can focus best. Take a pen and paper with you, and meditate on what you want, welcoming any idea that pops in your mind. Think and focus for fifteen, thirty minutes, one hour, or two, until it comes to you. Once you realise what your dreams are, every day when you wake up and before you go to sleep, think for five to ten minutes on what you want to accomplish and what you would like to do. Kindly ask your subconscious mind to guide you towards your calling and you will not fail.

We all had dreams when we were kids. See if you can remember them and you will understand what you want in this life. If you have new ideas or things that you think to be your calling, I suggest you give them a try. How else can you find out if it is something that you would like to do for the rest of your life?

There are three types of goals. Long-term goals often relate to having a family and financial freedom. As for the medium-term goals, these might regard learning a new language and taking various courses. Last, but not least, you have short-term goals, which must be accomplished on a daily or weekly basis.

The latter are essential because they will help you build consistency. They can become part of your self-worth building pillars, of which we spoke of earlier in this chapter. Thanks to them, you can gain focus and discipline. Let's take an example, such as going to the gym. Choose a goal like going to the gym five, six, or even seven days per week, following the routine of Arnold Schwarzenegger. Your motivation can be anything, as long, as it will help you carry on.

Your self-esteem will increase, as you will see the progress made with your own eyes, feeling happier and healthier as a result. After you set your goals, make sure that you make a program for anything you want to obtain. Promise yourself that no matter how hard it will get along the way, you will never give up. It is very important to understand that successful persons have their own mantra, one they repeat it to themselves, at least two or three times per day. This habit helps them imprint it into their subconscious, so that it becomes part of them.

Here is an example of how you can set your goals. Try to create your own and make sure to read it every day.

"My life's purpose is to (write your own goals) and in exchange for the joys of life, I will offer the best possible services, so that those who receive them will be satisfied." (Sign yourself)

I will make a diagram as an example on how to apply discipline. You can adjust it according to your needs, so that you can attain your goals. Say goodbye to procrastination and replace it with discipline. A bad habit is the one in which you come home from work, only to eat and watch TV. You should change this habit, for your own good. I haven't watched TV in over ten years and trust me when I say that I've never been happier to stay away from it. The following program will work, helping you become a better person, no matter who or what you think you are, a student, a 9-to-5 worker, or a parent with children. In the end, success occurs when dreams are bigger that excuses. Below, you will find several time management schedules for your daily routine.

We all have twenty-four hours in a day, the only difference between those who succeed and those who are poor is how they manage and use their given time. In the following pages, I will share personal development programs for beginners, intermediate, and advanced. As you will see, some are designed for the Monday to Friday intervals, while others are created for the weekend.

Keep in mind that these programs resemble the ones used by the army quite a lot. I haven't included simple actions, such as using the bathroom or brushing your teeth. I encourage you to use your common sense and apply it as you want. It might interfere with your schedule, but we are not machines, having to do everything minute by minute, and hour by hour. Your schedule should be done in such a way that it is sustainable on a long-term run. Thus, you won't consume all your energy. If that should happen, then be sure to rest, because every hard-working person deserves breaks. Resting is also part of self-love.

I know that these schedules are generally more suited for overachievers and high-performance people, but anyone can adjust them to their own needs. The most important thing is to follow a discipline, according to your requirements. If it's not going to help you long term, then you are wasting your time. Be careful what you wish for when you set your goals, to achieve your dreams. You will need to live up to the expectations of your needs when they become real. Remember, these schedules are not for time wasters. Every hour counts, especially when you have to work for somebody else. Your time is precious, and if you waste it, take responsibility for your situation, and get back on track. There is no need for judgement, we all fail occasionally. Nobody is perfect, but we must be disciplined if we want to achieve anything in life.

Samples

You have a chart box each at the end of the book.

Personal development program for beginners, Monday to Friday, by Adrian Vallace

WAKE-UP TIME AM	TO DO	NOTES
6 to 6.30	Meditation (to set your balance for the day ahead of you)	Drink water/Meditate for 10 – 15 minutes
6.30 to 7	Workout/ yoga/ box/ aerobics/ running. Any sort of physical exercise that resonates with you	Always stretch 5 minutes before working out / Exercise for 20-30 minutes
7 to 7.30	Shower/ eat/ journal (must have a to do list for the week)/ and write down what are you grateful for every day	Allocate 30 minutes
7.30 to 8	Read books/ online/YouTube or anything that gets you closer to your goals	Allocate 30 minutes

8 to 8.15	Get ready for work	Allocate 15 minutes
8 to 9	Travel/ drive/ cycle to work	1 hour depending on workplace distance/adjust if longer
8 to 9	If driving or cycling, listen to podcasts If commuting via trains or subways, read books	If that's not possible, work on your to-do list, see that you stay focused, so that you remember what needs to be done/make those phone calls, etc.
9 to 17	Work	Don't waste lunch time
13 to 14	Lunch/30 minutes eating. 10 minutes meditate. 20 minutes read/work on your diary for the day	When you are in a tight financial situation, the last thing you want is inadequate time management
	Repeat the 8 - 9 am travelling routine	Repeat
18 to 18.30	Take care of yourself after a hard day of work, shower, eat, cook, etc,	Self-care
18.30 to 20	If you have kids, spend time with them	Family time
18.30 to 20	If you don't have kids or any other people to take care of, you already know by now, work towards your dreams	Whatever you want to learn or become, study, or practice it, every day, for at least one hour

20 to 21	If you have a hobby, practice it. Try to stay off your phone, laptop, tv, with at least two hours before going to bed.	1 hour violin/ painting/ creativity Take a walk-in nature, talk to friends or family
21 to 21.30	Get ready to settle for the day and rest	Your healthy version of resting/ read/ watch a movie, just make sure you feed your brain positivity before sleep every night
21.30 to 22	Closing meditation	20 - 30 minutes meditate

Intermediate personal development program, Monday to Friday, by Adrian Vallace

WAKE UP TIME AM	TO DO	NOTES
5 to 5.30	Meditation (to set your balance for the day ahead of you)	Meditate for 20-30 minutes
5.30 to 6	Stretch/ physical exercise of your choice	Stretch 5 minutes/ exercise 25 minutes
6 to 6.30	Journaling Things you are grateful for every day / introspection/ daily goal	Consult your to do list 30 min

6.30 to 7	Get ready for work	Shower/ eat
7 to 8	Travel/ drive/ cycle	To work
7 to 8	If driving or cycling, listen to podcasts. If commuting via trains or subways, read books	1 hour, depending on the workplace distance
8 to 17	Work	Don't waste lunch time
13 to 14	Lunch/30 minutes eating 10 minutes meditate. 20 minutes read/ work on your diary for the day	Eat for 30 minutes, then take a walk/ meditate/ listen to something positive/ your choice
17 to 18	Repeat 7 – 8 am travelling routine	Repeat
18 to 19	Cooking/showering	Self-care
19 to 20	If you have kids, spend time with them	Family time
19 to 20	If you don't have kids or any other people to take care of, work on your dreams	Whatever you want to learn or become, study, or practice it every day, for at least one hour

20 to 21	If you have a hobby, practice it, if not, keep on working on your dreams	Personal development
21 to 22	Get ready to settle for the day/ rest. Call family or friends/ wife/ husband, etc.	Your healthy version of resting/ read/ watch a movie, just make sure you feed your brain positivity before sleep every night
22 to 22.30	Closing meditation (you need to balance your energy after a whole day filled with emotions and energies)	30 minutes meditate

Advanced personal development program, Monday to Friday, by Adrian Vallace

WAKE UP TIME AM	TO DO	NOTES
4 to 4.30	Meditation (to set your balance for the day ahead of you)	Drink water/30 minutes meditate
4.30 to 5.30	Workout/ yoga/ box/ aerobics/ running. Any sort of physical exercise that resonates with you	Stretch 5 to 10 minutes /1 hour exercise

5.30 to 6	Shower/ eat/ journal (must have a to-do list for the week)/ write down what are you grateful for every day	Allocate 30 minutes
6 to 6.45	Read books/ online/ YouTube, or anything that gets you closer to your goals	Allocate 45 minutes
6.45 to 7	Get ready for work	Allocate 15 minutes
7 to 8	Travel/drive/cycle to work	1 hour depending on the workplace distance. If more, adjust accordingly
7 to 8	If driving or cycling, listen to podcasts If commuting via trains or subways, read books	If that's not possible, work on your to-do list, see that you stay focused, so that you remember what needs to be done/make those phone calls, etc.
8 to 17	Work	Don't waste lunch time
13 to 14	Lunch/30 minutes eating 10 minutes meditate. 20 minutes read/ work on your diary for the day	When you are in a tight financial situation, the last thing you want is inadequate time management
17 to 18	Repeat the 7 - 8 am traveling routine	Repeat

18 to 18.30	Take care of yourself after a hard day of work, shower, eat, etc.	Self-care
18.30 to 20	If you have kids, spend time with them	Family time
18.30 to 20	If you don't have kids, or any other people to take care of you already know by now, work towards your dreams	Whatever you want to learn or become, study, or practice it every day for at least one hour
20 to 21	If you have a hobby, practice it	1 hour violin/ painting/ creativity Take a walk-in nature, talk to friends or family
21 to 22	Get ready to settle for the day and rest	Your healthy version of resting/ read/ watch a movie, just make sure you feed your brain positivity before sleep every night
22 to 22.30	Closing meditation	30 minutes meditate

    Once you have found a balance in your daily routine, which should cover at least the essentials – health (physical, mental, and emotional), finances, relationships, career, contribution to society, all will fall into place and the universe will get out of your way. You will be able to create your own path, your own life legend, as Paulo Coelho so wonderfully says in "The Alchemist".

    Next, we are going to do a weekend schedule for personal development. If you work during the weekend, you will have to rest throughout the week, otherwise you will burn out quickly. If you work only on Saturday, take the entire Sunday off. Just relax and restore your body. But if you work on both Saturday and Sunday, choose two days during the week, and take a break from your routine. The following schedule is for those who do not work on weekends. I suggest that you sleep a bit more during the weekend, so that both your mind and body are rested and thus balanced.

Personal development schedule, Saturday

WAKE UP TIME AM	TO DO	NOTES
7 to 7.30	Meditate	Meditate in bed for 30 minutes, lying down or sitting with crossed legs
7.30 to 8.30	Read anything that helps you focus on your business/ dreams/ personal development / spirituality	Make a cup of tea or coffee, and read for an hour
8.30 to 9	Stretch and get ready for your chosen workout or running routine	Stretch for 10 minutes
9 to 10	Workout/ running/ yoga, etc.	Keep your body fit

10 to 11	Breakfast and relaxation	Breakfast
11 to 15	House chores/ shopping/ cleaning/ cooking/ washing, etc.	Four hours of chores
15 to 16	Read/ write/ study/ research for your business	One more hour of personal development
16 onwards free time to do whatever you want	It's time to take a break for the rest of the day. Remember to meditate before sleep	Relax/ go out/ watch a movie/ go on a date/ spend time with family, etc.
Try not to sleep later than midnight, to keep your body balanced	Try not to go to sleep later than midnight. The earlier you sleep, the easier it will be to wake up	Sleeping helps with productivity

Personal development schedule, Sunday

WAKE UP TIME AM	TO DO	NOTES

8 to 8.30	Meditate	Always find time to meditate
8.30 to 9.30	Read anything that helps you focus on your business/ dreams/ personal development / spirituality	Reading helps the mind grow and stay focused
9.30 to 10	Stretch and get ready for your chosen workout	Stretch
10 to 11	Workout/ running/yoga, etc.	If you work out daily, you can take Sunday off
11 to 12	Brunch	Take a break and have your brunch
12 onwards free time to do whatever you want	Take your time and get yourself ready for the following week	Do your to-do lists or the short- and medium-term goals to stay focused
All afternoon	Relax however you want	Relax

22.00 Try to be in bed by ten pm so that you're ready for the following week.	Always be in bed by ten pm on Sunday, so you're rested for next week, and remember to meditate before sleeping	Go to bed by 10 pm. Meditate at least 20 minutes

    I know this might be a harsh schedule, but if you summon the courage to get through a couple of months, I bet you will see major changes and improvements in your health, focus, and emotional balance. Then, if you managed to follow the program for a month or two, challenge yourself to push through six months, then one year. And if you don't like what you've become within a year, you can just drop it. But at least this much you owe to yourself, to see how much you can grow in a year by being disciplined. Once successful, you can turn it into a lifestyle, as you desire.

CHAPTER 6

LEARN HOW TO REWARD YOURSELF

Learn how to forgive yourself; when you lose or make mistakes, and learn from experience.

> "The reward of a good deed is to have done it." (Seneca)

What is a reward? A reward is something given or received in recognition or appreciation of one's efforts, achievements, or contributions. A reward can take many forms, such as financial compensation (bonus or salary increase), non-financial recognition (honours or awards), or intrinsic benefit (personal satisfaction or a sense of accomplishment). Rewards can be used to motivate and encourage desired behaviours or outcomes. They can be valuable tools to promote employee engagement and job satisfaction. Rewarding yourself is a great way to acknowledge your accomplishments and maintain motivation towards achieving your goals.

Here are six bullet points on how to reward yourself:

1. Set achievable goals. Choose realistic goals for yourself and break them down into smaller milestones. This will help you stay motivated and give you something to work towards.

2. Decide your reward. Choose a reward that you will enjoy and that is in line with your goals. For example, if your goal is to exercise more, your reward could be a massage or a new workout outfit.

3. Celebrate your accomplishments. When you reach a milestone or achieve a goal, take the time to celebrate your accomplishment. This will help you stay motivated and reinforce positive behaviour.

4. Make it meaningful. Make sure your reward is something that is meaningful to you and will inspire you to continue working towards your goals.

5. Be consistent. Set a schedule for rewarding yourself and stick to it. This will help you stay motivated and create a sense of routine.

6. Avoid self-destructive rewards. Avoid using food, alcohol, or other self-destructive behaviours as rewards. Instead, choose rewards that will have a positive impact on your physical or mental health. Remember, rewarding yourself is a great way to stay motivated and achieve your goals, but it's important to choose rewards that are in line with your values and goals. Choose rewards that will help you maintain a healthy and balanced lifestyle.

Remember when you were a kid, and whenever you did something good or productive, you would get a reward? For instance, you helped an old lady cross the street. A reward motivates you to do wonderful things for you and those around you. It comes as a form of positive reinforcement, helping people thrive. There were times we did something, let's just call it "bad" for the sake of old mentalities. For example, we might have tried to dismantle a toy and then attempted to put it back. Well, if you had parents like mine, that would have been seen as something negative. My dad used to call me a "destroyer", threatening that he will never buy anything for me. That is how you kill the creativity and confidence of a child; the negative reinforcement psychologists speak of nowadays.

Now, we all know, especially the new-age parents, that I wasn't just dismantling a toy, but my creative mind was curious to see what it was made of, or what was inside it. It's vital to remember that we don't have control on what happens around us, and that sometimes things will not go our way or how we have planned, which will lead to disappointment. In times like this, it's best to keep your calm and don't even think about blaming or beating yourself up. Failures help us grow exponentially, if we learn from them and remember they are part of life.

Most of us have beaten ourselves up, for not being able to bow down to society's requirements at some point in our lives, whether it was related to work, school, or our personal relationships. Maybe our boss told us that we weren't good enough. Or the same words were uttered by our teachers, or even worse, our parents. If we look back in time, such words didn't help or worked for us in any way. However, with the passing of time, we managed to let go. For some, it was easier, for others, harder. Some of us may still be clinging to those words.

Now, as grown-ups, we are in charge of how we feel, and we get to decide whether we let anything negative break through our energy field. We can simply detach, removing ourselves from those people or circumstances, and choosing to stay positive. Our thoughts influence over mentality and vice-versa. Never underestimate yourself, because you can do extraordinary things and no matter what the situation is, if you keep your calm and focus, you will make it.

As you are following your schedule, there will be many times where you will feel like giving up. If you also suffer from ADHD, like I do, you will start many projects and not finish any of them. You might simply feel like you are tired, losing your focus, lacking the desire to pursue your goals. To maintain your focus, you need to stay healthy. Stay away from fast food and other unhealthy foods, drink only water and herbal teas, exercise daily, meditate regularly, and take cold showers to keep your immune system strong. Work on yourself, as this can help you start your business or improve it.

Once you add all of these to your routine, it will be difficult to lose your focus. Every one of these little things that you do, will allow you to create a better self, becoming a pillar, like the ones mentioned earlier. If you want to get your dopamine levels up, so that you stay productive, you must have clear goals to focus on. Keep them pinned up on a wall, so that you can see them every day, in the living room, at your desk. You might also have affirmations in your bathroom, reading them daily, as they will also help you stay focused. You can look online and print several, then stick them on your mirror. As you brush your teeth in the morning, you can read affirmations for self-love, life's purpose, abundance, prosperity, inner clarity, peace, and gratefulness. Louise Hay has great affirmations; I encourage you to give her a try.

In the morning, when you wake up, the first thing to say before getting out of your bed should be a repetitive mantra, such as "today, I will create a day full of love, abundance, and prosperity". Repeat it at least five to ten times each morning, adapting it to your needs and wants. If you have an exam, on that day you can say "today, I will take and pass the exam easily and effortlessly". You can then repeat it in your meditation as well.

At night, after your meditation or prayer, before you put your head on the pillow, repeat this mantra five to ten times. "Tonight, I will fall asleep calmly, easily, and peacefully, and in the morning, I will wake up well rested and ready for a new day". A great way to keep your dopamine levels up, so that you can stay productive, is to complete at least two or three things from your to-do list per day. Each evening, you need to keep yourself accountable for the three things you have achieved, and for which you are grateful to have happened.

By doing so, you are telling your brain that you are an achiever, which will be interpreted as positive feedback. As a result, you will increase both your self-esteem and self-worth on a long-term basis. This is a very healthy way to reward yourself biologically. At the end of each week, or at least one time per month, buy yourself something nice or go out to a nice restaurant to celebrate your achievements. This is another way of celebrating the good things in your life. The best way to reward yourself is by doing what you love the most, like a hobby that you have, but can't do it very often, due to the present situation you are in.

"Forgiving yourself allows clear energy to flow through your body." (Adrian Lungu)

Some people need to learn how to take a break. You know, I am talking about those people who have a day off, but you see them around the house, building a little cat or doghouse, or fixing things that aren't a priority. Those people don't really know how to enjoy themselves, that's why you always see them doing things. They find hard to stay still or relax. This is a conditioning that has been created during their childhood by teachers or parents, people who would say things like "while you take a break, why don't you take out the rubbish or sweep the floor". In doing so, they turned into perfectionists, and never seem to enjoy a break, all due to their conditioning.

The reason I am sharing this is because I have been there. I needed to learn how to take breaks and reward myself. Therapy helped me to understand that what I was doing should not be compared with somebody else's work, and that we all have our own pace of doing things. I learned that if I wanted to get far, I should take my time and be consistent. Being in a "doing" mode all the time, with hyperactivity, would lead to burnout. I learned this lesson the hard way, for many years in a row.

So, I had to learn to take a day or even a weekend off from my routine, and I went out more often as well. Regardless of what I was doing, if I enjoyed it, and it allowed me to separate myself from my daily routine, it was a reward. I managed to replace my old conditioning, outdated beliefs, with a new and healthy mindset, having understood how important it was to reward and enjoy myself.

Mistakes will be made, and I have made tons, God is my witness, but we must understand how important mistakes are for our growth. Let's say you want to start a new business. Everyone makes mistakes it the beginning, they are part of our growth journey. By doing things the wrong way, you will learn not to repeat the mistakes made again. And even if you do repeat them, eventually you will learn the necessary lessons the hard way. You are the one getting burned, but that's what is going to help you grow.

When making mistake, the most important thing is to put not too much pressure on yourself. Blaming yourself is not good, as the self-guilt will eventually wear you out over time, mentally, emotionally, and most possibly, physically. So, whenever you make a mistake, try to change your perception, and look at the positive side of it. It is also important not to attach yourself to physical objects. Such an attitude will help the brain to repair what is broken with ease, as opposed to the situation in which you are angry and annoyed.

I think we can all agree that when we are angry, we can't fix things. Everything goes downhill instead. Generally speaking, by shifting your perception, you will ease your life. The lesson here should be that you understand how important making mistakes is for your growth. You should also learn how to forgive yourself, without attaching yourself to the situation. Forgiving yourself allows clear energy to flow through your body, and when energy flows through you with ease, your life will be a smooth ride.

We all have a non-judgemental side, but it can be hard to tap into it and forgive ourselves. This is not an easy task, sometimes it is harder than forgiving others. You must address your compassionate side, something which can be done through regular practice. Do this imagination exercise as often as possible. Close your eyes and imagine a person of your own choice, a man or a woman, somebody who could handle situations that you are not able to.

Here is an example. You get into a heated argument with someone, knowing that it won't end well for either of you. Think of a person that would know how to deal with that situation at its best, whether that person is a friend, a family member, or even an imaginary person created in your mind. Ask that person what I should do and how should I behave or interact, or what kind of action should you take.

I personally have two imaginary models in my mind. When I'm in great need, I rely on their advice. The first is an old man with a white beard and a staff, which is the pen he uses to write in the Akashic records. He can access everything that has been written. We seem to always meet on top of a mountain, on a rock where it is nice and quiet. Whenever I am in a pickle, I ask him for advice and wisdom. I also have a compassionate old lady. She doesn't really have a face, for whatever reason I could not attach a face to her. But she always wears a scarf over her head, just like all the old ladies do. Whenever I am in pain or I need a compassionate shoulder, someone to listen to, she is always there. She soothes me and tells me everything will be all right, whilst I have my head on her lap, her hands caressing my head like a loving grandmother. So, you can have as many imaginary persons as you want, ready to guide you.

I would like to tell you about a book called "Life Changing Secrets from the Three Masters of Success: 3 Habits to Achieve Abundance in Your Finances, Your Health and Your Life". It was co-authored by Napoleon Hill, Dale Carnegie, and Joseph Murphy. Napoleon Hill mentions how he used to have a big round table, where some of the greatest minds of our time gathered, like Einstein, Napoleon, or Abraham Lincoln. He would talk to them and ask for advice. The more he did it, the clearer his visualisations became, up to the point where they had conversations daily.

Now think about it for a minute. These people are the grandfathers of personal development. They learned to master their subconscious during some of the harshest times of the past hundred years. They lived through the Holocaust, Hitler's reign of terror, hunger, and harsh diseases, both World War I and II, governmental hits, financial crises, and crashes. If you were you research them, you would discover that they weren't doing bad for their time, whereas their business, financial independence, and emotional health were concerned.

I studied some of the greats, and the most common denominator that I found was that they never blamed the country they lived in or the family they grew up with or without. They did not blame their sex or race either. They all had this in common. When it comes to the recipe for success, this is the main ingredient. Think about it, here we are fifty or a hundred years later, and common sense tell me that we have advanced as human species, especially in the past fifty years. In turn, this comes as confirmation that we can do better.

Nowadays, if we want to visualise, we have audio and video available on our smartphones, or we can use virtual reality goggles. We can access any kind of information, thanks to the Internet. In addition, we can speak to anyone, from anywhere around the world. So, if you want a yoga teacher from India, no problem, you don't have to travel thousands of kilometres to get there. Or if you want a coach from Japan, boom, just open your laptop and have a video call.

Personally, I am not a visual person, because I had a rough childhood and I had to mature quickly. I wasn't allowed to daydream, I had to be on my toes constantly. As a result, I prefer physical touch. I must listen to guided meditations if I want to visualise or understand how to do it. What I am trying to say is that we have limitless possibilities. You can now go ahead and create as many imaginary friends as you want. Leave judgement aside, and don't let the past create your future.

I see how many kids are being stripped of their creativity and imagination in our society, where if a child has an imaginary friend, he/she is being reported to the school officials. The other kids are being taught to judge by their parents after a certain age. They learn from their behaviour, as kids can be quite observant. Remember, kids are like sponges up until the age of seven, they record and remember everything quite easily. Naturally, that reflects in their life and at school. Kids aren't mean, they are just an extension of their environment. So remember that judgement kills creativity, and without imagination, we cannot create all these beautiful things that you see around us. Let us tap into our creative ideas and imagination, creating our own mental palaces and imaginary friends.

By now, you have probably understood that this chapter focuses on rewards. I am trying to show you how to reward yourself. Maybe you are like me, and your rewarding system comes from the past. I used to "reward" myself by intoxicating my mind and body. Well, maybe it's time you think of an imaginary person, someone who will teach you how to reward yourself, having your best interest at heart.

I hope you have learned how to reward and forgive yourself, acting with compassion, love, and kindness. Let's talk about how we can learn from our mistakes. I will give you a few examples from my own experience. It all started when I was a teenager. I drank alcohol and smoked cigarettes with my friends, going to a club for the first time, despite being only 13 years old. By the time I was in my twenties, I was a professional drinker, close to an alcoholic. The years went by and I ended up even worse.

The six years I spent in Cyprus only made by addiction worse. I was young and my entourage had similar habits. We were all drinking, smoking, and doing drugs. You know the saying "birds of a feather flock together"? There I was, drinking vodka, beer, red wine, tequila. I behaved just like any other young man in his twenties, pouring my guts out almost every night. It did not take long until I moved up, starting to abuse pills, cocaine, LSD, and any other drug that would come my way. I was the guy who would just take something right then and there, asking later about its effect. And so, I've spent almost fifteen years of my life, the years where I should've been enjoying my youth.

Until one day, when I looked at myself in the mirror, with great disgust. I didn't like what and who I saw. And even though those were some of the worst years of my life, after reflecting on that time, with many deep introspections, I have come toa significant conclusion. Those experiences have taught me some of the greatest lessons, lessons that probably a parent would teach his kids. I have learned what not to do. I am forever grateful to have had those experiences in my youth, that they didn't occur later in life.

The last thing I would want to happen is to turn fifty, and start smoking, drinking, and doing cocaine. When you are in your twenties, you can do drugs and drink, then go to work, to the gym, make love to your girlfriend several times a day, because you have that kind of energy. But after forty, your level of energy is not the same, and the recovery from is harder. This is my biggest lesson for you to remember. If you want to try things, try them while you're young. You will have the advantage of a speedy recovery.

Choose your entourage wisely, your group of friends should be in alignment with your dreams. I had to learn this lesson the hard way, because alcoholic friends are not to be trusted and there is no honour within such a group. No one talks about how low your self-esteem is, after all those years of intoxication. We don't talk about how much work we had to do, to become sober and get back into society.

I was always relying on alcohol as a friend, to be able to speak in public or maintain a relationship. It might take years for you to recover and regain your self-worth. It is almost like being a prostitute for ten years, and then wanting to become a respectable woman. You will need years of therapy just to learn how not to judge yourself and start loving yourself unconditionally. Therapy will also help you understand why you must change your surroundings and move away from the group of people who used to humour your behaviour when intoxicated.

Such changes will require going out of your comfort zone quite a lot, but with a heavy luggage. It can be done, but the more you leave it, the harder it will be. For me, all those years of creating negative habits turned out to be of great value, but only because of my new perspective and the ten years of personal development. I had to learn how to break through negative thinking patterns, addictions, and victimisation behaviours. And I am still working to create new habits and heal, as I have decided to make personal development a lifestyle and not just a six-month course on how to turn my life around.

Life has taught me how to create space. I also discovered that even a small action can have a massive impact on the world. Just like the butterfly effect. Here it is. I will start this by saying how when I was a kid, my dad used to tell me how he stole shoes from his old factory and sell them on the black market during the communist era. Back then, life was hard and so much more different than nowadays. He would share so many stories that they eventually became part of my teenage early education years.

I remember that first time I ever stole something, when I was about eight years old. It was at the playground, behind our block of flats. I used to play with two twin brothers, and one day, I asked from one of them if I could have his watch. Then, I just pretended that I lost it and ran away. We eventually split up, and a few hours later, I was back at the playground. I could see from afar how my twin friends were coming towards me, together with their mom. I realized that they had snitched on me.

As she was approaching, I felt threatened and started to run away. When I looked back, their mom was running hard to get me. I started running, without ever turning my head back, for a few blocks until I lost her. Mind you, she was a woman in her mid-thirties, and I don't think she was coming to kick my ass. But I was too young and too scared, and to be honest, I was never the kind to just sit tight, whenever a threat approached me.

And so, I managed to get home, and got all settled in. I was playing with my new watch, and about one or two hours later, I heard a knock on the door. My mom opened the door and guess who was there, our neighbour friend, the one who was chasing me earlier. She had come with one of the twins, from which I had stolen the watch. As you can very well understand, my mom told me to give the watch back and she apologised, after scolding me in front of them, with that old motherly saying "how could you do this to me".

Anyway, this was the beginning of my journey. I went from stealing a little toy to becoming a kleptomaniac, and this affected me so much in life. I was stealing food from markets, and pretty much anything from various workplaces, obviously to an extent that wouldn't get noticed. It went the same until one day. I was working on a building site. Me and my business partner were hired as contractors, and we had to finish between eight and twelve houses, acting as both house painters and decorators. I had enough money, but being a kleptomaniac is a disease and it is quite hard to recover.

So here I was, wandering on the site, when I saw a pair of red pliers on the floor. I simply picked the pliers and put them in my backpack. A couple of hours passed by, and we were getting ready to have our lunch break. As I was heading towards the cafeteria, I heard this guy on the site screaming and cursing, up and down, and left and right. He kept repeating that he was unable to find his special pair of pliers, the ones he used to open the doors with.

As I heard him from afar, something awakened inside, a voice that said, "this is it, we cannot do this anymore", because I had finally understood how the butterfly effect would work in real life. What to me did not even mean that much, had created a big stressful situation, not just for one, but for more people. I talked to my best friend and business partner about what had happened at lunch time. I looked him right in the eyes and swore that I will never ever steal or touch anything that doesn't belong to me, for the rest of my life. He behaved like a great friend and kept me accountable for the following years that we worked together.

The lesson for me has been clear. Not only did I understand the impact a small action can have and how much damage can be done when redirected with a negative focus, but I have also learned a more spiritual lesson. I have learned how to create space for abundance. You see, when I was stealing all those little things, a tool from work, or a t-shirt, the message that I was sending out into the universe was that I stole because I didn't have enough. It had become a vicious, never-ending circle. Once I stopped that negative thinking pattern and those actions, I started to create space for healthy wealth in my life, which I hope to pass to the next generation.

I hope that through these few life lessons, I was able to make you aware as well. Some time ago, a wise person said that a clever man learns from his mistakes, but a wise man learns from someone else's mistakes. So here I am, sharing some of mine, in the hope that it will serve future generations. I could write more about this, but then we will take this book to a whole different philosophical level, and that is not my purpose here. Maybe on my next book, I will expand more on psychological behaviours and life patterns. I will conclude this part with a personal quote.

"If you won't take care of yourself in this life, nobody will. Find your path and become your greatest version."

CHAPTER 7

PERSISTENCE AND MOTIVATION

"Three things are essential: patience, persistence, and consistency."

Nowadays, in our society, motivation is an overrated movement, a concept too often used. Yet, given our conditioning and the lack of guidance during childhood, it has become necessary. That is why we have such a big number of procrastinators, as well as people who give up so easily on their dreams, when they haven't even reached the age of twenty-five. There is also a lack of patience involved, which we subliminally receive, mostly from mass media. They are selling fake dreams and fake identities, with their fake adverts, which make people believe they are not good enough and how,
they need to buy this to have that, or to be like this to look a certain way.

The AI technology is getting better and better at pattern recognition, monitoring people's desires 24/7. That is why kids want everything fast, one day delivery, six-pack abs in 4 weeks, and a million pounds in their account within a few days, because they are being told that they too can have what they want, if they buy this or that, and nobody else wants to do the real work anymore. They foolishly fall into this trap. But if you were to study the greats of the world, paying attention to their programme and discipline, you would understand there is no shortcut to success.

Successful people wake up early and go to work, even though they don't need it anymore. They have enough money to retire, but for them work represents a lifestyle, a way of living. It's about leaving a legacy, not about making it happen anymore. So, if you want success and personal development, I am talking about lifetime dedication, not just a couple of months or a year. A lifetime of building and developing a great character, helping your community, family, and friends.

To be motivated in life, you must know where you are heading. You must have clear goals, and these should make you feel good. You must enjoy the journey, otherwise you will give up easily and not only that. Because maybe you will not give up, but you won't be fulfilled, and that is our holy grail in life, our main priority and goal, finding out what we love doing and never stopping until we have achieved it.

Life will inevitable get hard, with obstacles along the way. Terrible things will happen, people dear to us will die, accidents might occur. We can lose our marriage, our house, our money. Or we might have an accident, which can break out body in unimaginable ways. And because we are emotional beings, this will traumatise us. That is our life test, that is a moment in life, when you not only have to go through pain, you have to push and grow through it, even if the pain its unbearable, even if you need to cry and let go of what no longer serves you, like the anger, the pain, the shame.

Take time to recover and rebalance, but make sure you don't remain in that place, because it is very easy to become a victim, and that is the last place on your emotional scale that you want to be, after you've encountered a life struggle. Playing the role of a victim can drag you down very much, way beneath being homeless. And not only you will no longer be in control of your mind, but all that negative energy will vibrate on a lower level of consciousness. Instead, understand life goes on, no matter what. And you are responsible for every choice that you decide to take or not.

Some experiences in life can never be forgotten. However, it is entirely our choice how we decide to feel at any time. If someone dear to us, like a family member were to die, that event would become a life-lasting memory and experience. But I could assure you that if the respective person loved you, he or she would wish for you to start your life over again. Nobody said anything about forgetting, but if you still carry traumas caused by past experiences, there are many techniques out there that can help you achieve emotional balance, like the emotional freedom technique, meditation, different types of therapies, Wim Hof techniques, and many others which you will find presented in the emotional freedom chapter.

No matter what happens in our life, there are no excuses if we don't try, if we don't push ourselves. We cannot ask ourselves why we haven't made it, if we didn't even try, if we gave up just because life happened. There are so many examples out there. People who never gave up, despite life hitting them hard, people who have managed to thrive in life and serve as great examples. Take Nick Vujicic, a man born without arms or legs. He is a painter, swimmer, skydiver, and motivational speaker. He is 40 years old as I am writing this book. He was born with an extremely rare congenital disorder known as Phocomelia, which is characterised by the absence of legs and arms. This guy is a swimmer and a painter, guys, what is your excuse? And more importantly, if you have one, why do you have one? He has written eight books and God knows that he isn't done. He is only in the midst of his life and is able to inspire millions of people around the world, me included.

Excuses represent nothing more than conditioning beliefs, which we repeated in our minds for so many times that they changed our reality. At the core of such beliefs lies a deep, unconscious fear. This fear has created who you are right now, but the good news is that it can be changed, through deep introspection and powerful motivation.

Let's take an example. A person is overweight, and he or she has had this problem for their entire life, let's say for the past twenty years or so. Nowadays, everybody knows that to lose weight you need to do just a few things, like exercising and watching your diet. But knowing these solutions is not enough, because there might be an emotional, traumatic wound behind it. To find more about this, you can read the book written by Lise Bourebeau, "The five wounds'". I will also explain a little bit about it here.

Not only do I understand the struggle of what it is like to lack the motivation for getting up early and going for a run, but I understand the emotional science behind it. First, being overweight brings more than fat cells that won't go away easily. The emotional trauma experienced in childhood often has to do with humiliation. The poor child feels like one of his/her parents, usually the mother, is ashamed of them. One might consider the child is dirty or too messy in public. Therefore, the child will start to feel ashamed and judged. As a result, their body will begin to accumulate fat, at first to hide their genitals from their parents, due to an increasing lack of confidence. Along the way, they will experience a lot of embarrassing situations, which they will attract unconsciously throughout their lifetime. But this can be healed.

I would suggest you read the book written by Lise Bourebeau. It is called "Heal Your Wounds and Find Your True Self", and trust me, going to therapy for more than two years or enrolling into a psychology course will not teach you what such books can. Now, after the overweight person has managed to cover their emotional luggage, which is not easy work but can be done, through raising one's awareness, they can start making different decisions for their wellbeing. They might adopt a vegetarian or vegan lifestyle, to stop consuming unnecessary fats, coming from the meat that is being sold in today's markets.

Then, they can quit sugar, especially the one that comes from processed products. Sugar has a powerful addictive effect and is on the same chart as heroin when it comes to addiction levels. The next step would be to stop smoking or drinking, provided such negative habits are present. Once these things are gradually achieved, one can start going to the gym or develop an exercise routine, as this is going to help them become fit. One must take these physical steps and understand they shouldn't care what other people think about them or their change, otherwise change is going to be impossible.

But if one understands that what other people think about them is not their reality, they could become the one thing which most are probably afraid of, which is free. Free of what others think, like their friends or family, who can be quite judgmental. Free of the trauma that causes them to carry such a heavy load within their body. Free of addictions, such as sugar and negative thinking, the latter clouding the judgement and clarity we require for our mental focus and emotional wellbeing.

A good start would be to detach from people and experiences that do not serve them in any way. And I know that fear is holding a lot of people back from taking action, the fear of how people might laugh at them, for instance, for not being able to run in a certain way, or the fear of others telling them they will never make it, and it will all lead to the deepest of fears, the fear of failure. What if I'm not going to make it, what if I can't do it, what if I break my legs, what if I fall... This is just the tip of the iceberg of the *what ifs*, which blocks your progress and keeps the self-esteem at the lowest possible level.

You must stand in front of the mirror and talk to yourself, the harshest critic, who is also the strongest person in your life. Who is that person? You are! Ask yourself how long your mind, body, and spirit will be able to take this. Say "no more, I deserve to be strong, healthy, and worthy of achieving my dreams". State this every morning when you wake up, tell yourself how strong you want to become and how high you are willing to climb the ladder of your own success. Say out loud, "I will no longer be controlled by outside entities, and I am taking control over my own destiny", "no heart aches and diseases have dominion over my cells", "I am grateful that my subconscious is healing my body with every passing second". Repeat these phrases every morning, as many times as possible. Look deeply into your own eyes, until you feel the dopamine levels going up, so that you feel capable to act and go out for a run, for instance.

If you know exactly what action you need to take for your health, but you still won't do it, do not despair. You are not alone. What happens is that the reptilian brain acts in opposition to the prefrontal cortex, the latter being responsible for our decisions. For the prefrontal cortex to win, a lot of persistence is required. You need to push yourself daily. No matter how many times you have started something, only to give up, dust yourself off and try again. Keep at it until you rewire your brain.

Our brain presents a unique ability, which is called neuroplasticity. Thanks to this ability, we can rewire, recondition, or reprogram our brain. Scientists have discovered that if you want to implement a new healthy habit, the brain needs repetitive actions taken by the body and the nervous system. That represents an evolutionary discovery. However, please do not expect for twenty years of bad habits to be changed within a couple of weeks. Patience, persistence, and consistency are key elements when it comes to achieving long-lasting motivation. Once achieved, this will become another pillar for your healthy habits, which in turn will help you change your life for the better. Let's break them down, so you can understand why and how they matter.

Why is patience essential? Well, if we won't develop patience along life experiences, then we will rush into things, wanting everything to happen faster and easier. Eventually, this will break us down, due to the expectations imposed by none other than ourselves. Rushing will make us take rushed decisions, which will not help us in the long run.

Let's say we want to lose 10 kilos, but we want to do that within a month. I'm not saying that is not possible. But if you've never worked out or ran in your life, and you are just starting, here is what is going to happen. You might attempt to go running for one hour, followed by a normal workout, which might extend up to two hours. Then, you might try to run again, for one hour in the afternoon. I can assure you that you will be disappointed, as you will feel exhausted. You might also injure yourself, wanting to quit, even though you are not even halfway in. One needs to be more realistic and follow a specific routine. This is valid not just for running. It should become a lifestyle and not something that you will end up doing for two months per year, for the rest of your life, expecting to be super fit. I know it is hard, but such lessons are essential in the long run.

Why is persistence significant? Its role comes into sight when we start a new routine. Persistent means to keep pushing, even if we don't feel like it or the outside world influences us. Let's say you run daily, and you catch a cold. Your nose is dripping, and you are coughing. Your mind will automatically activate your defence mechanism, doing its best to protect you. As a result, most likely you will encounter thoughts such as "I need to rest", "it's too cold", "my muscles hurt", and so on. Persistence is a mindset that helps you to go on, even if your conditioning is telling you not to. Do not give in. Try to understand that if you have a cold and go out for a run, you will improve your immune system. It might sound strange, but you will feel better after the run or workout, because your blood will get moving and your white cells will fight potential bacteria and viruses. Think of persistence as your very good friend, someone who only wants the best for you.

Why is consistency vital? One of the most common words that successful people use is *consistency*, because the repetitiveness of it will help one achieve his or her dreams. Through your wins and fails, it will be with you forever. Imagine running for thirty minutes, every day for the rest of your life. The data says that if you run every day, for at least twenty minutes, your life expectancy will increase with up to seven years. Now imagine that you add that consistency to your relationships, business, and personal life. In one year, you will be able to achieve what others achieve in five, only because you were consistent. So, don't ever give up, keep pushing until you can't do it anymore, and when you reach that point, keep going.

There are five essential steps that need to be taken to maintain your motivation.

Step no. 1

Set medium-term goals, write what you want to achieve within three to six months, whether you want to lose weight, get a raise, study more, develop your business, etc. First, we must start with a weekly to-do list, where we include even the most mundane tasks, such as doing the bed. Then, we will add more tasks, such as making uncomfortable phone calls or asking the boss for a raise. Once we complete these steps, our self-esteem will increase, and we will be able to handle more tasks over time. We will move towards our goals with ease, as our mind becomes gradually conditioned, and we tend to achieve everything with less effort. You should create a nice list and a vision board, adding your medium and long-term goals. The medium ones are those that can be achieved within three to six months, or even a year. Once you achieve these, think of some long-term goals, which might require five to ten years or even more, such as having a lovely family, buying the car you dreamed of, starting a company, buying a house for your family, or curing cancer.

Step no. 2

Start now. As a wise man once said, the best time to plant a tree was twenty-five years ago. But it's never too late, as twenty-five years from now, the tree would still have grown. It is the same with people. Maybe some don't need that much time to grow, but there's no such thing as too much wisdom. Once we have started, we must go on, until we find our momentum. After we have found it, it is like riding a wave, where you don't need to paddle that much anymore, as the wave is carrying you with ease. So imagine that you start a brand new workout, which is usually hard to grasp in the beginning and maybe even challenging. Two, three weeks, or even a month in, you will get the hang of it, and it will be much easier to train a month later than it was at first. With the passing of time, you will do it with a different mindset and passion, riding the wave of your own momentum.

Step no. 3

Acknowledge and celebrate your wins. If it gets hard or you feel like you can't do it anymore, just take breaks, as a well-earned break sometimes can be the key to great success. Let's say you're working on a project, and you get stuck, because maybe you haven't done enough research, or you are just too tired. Sometimes, to finish, the only thing you can do is to take a break. Relax your mind and body, because a rested mind usually produces better ideas, compared to a tired one. So, take a step back and relax. Assess the situation, and when you're ready, get back to it.

Step no. 4

People. Be very careful who you surround yourself with, as they will affect your work, business, and life experiences. If your friends are not in alignment or resonate with you, learn to detach yourself. Otherwise, it will cost you, and you will have to pay with one of your most precious currencies, meaning time. If your mates want to go down the pub two, three days per week, they obviously have the necessary financial stability or just don't care how such habits will affect the both of you in the next twenty to thirty years. When you'll be in your forties or fifties, instead of having your life together, you will still be at the pub, discussing somebody else's life, and how they made it. Remember that nobody cares or ever will, about you, the way that you do.

Step no. 5

Try and find somebody who is already successful at the thing you want to achieve. Follow the journey of that person or find yourself a mentor. Certain NFT techniques teach you that the fastest way to attain your goals is to try what somebody else is doing, with your own adaptation. This will help you reach the same amount of success. The main idea here is to never stop learning, whether you have a mentor, self-help books, or courses.

Eventually, we must learn how to turn our routine into a lifestyle. Otherwise, it will become hard to even wake up in the morning. But once we discover what we love to do the most, that inner passion will be our motivation. It will represent the persistence we need to keep pushing. We must find a way to love our daily routine. If you are a person who loves personal development, then this book is for you. But if you are not in this world of development, then it will be hard to break through and understand the importance of your routine. You need it to achieve what you want, better health, better finances, better emotional balance, better mental health, better relationships, better career opportunities.

All these things depend on choices that must be taken in our lifetime. As I said earlier in the book, you simply can't behave like the eighty percent of the population and expect the results of remaining twenty percent. Successful people never stop mentioning the importance of their routine. If they would've stopped their routine twenty years ago, they wouldn't have made it. And once they made it, they didn't stop. This was not because they couldn't, the respective routine turned into a lifestyle for them. They choose this conditioning, instead of their childhood, which had been programmed into their minds without them having a choice, as it happened for all of us.

If I would have chosen to stay as I was conditioned in my young age, by now, I would've have been a homeless alcoholic, probably sleeping on the street, with no job or money, and most probably taking any drug available at my disposal, just to run away from reality. Instead, I chose to recreate my reality and recondition my mind, and to regenerate my body and cells, so that every atom in my body works for me. I will go down this path, no matter how hard it is or will be for me to achieve my dreams. It is infinitely better to wake up at four am and go to the gym, than to wake up frozen on the street, on a piece of cardboard with just a blanket on, and full of negative thoughts. Let's be honest, it is very difficult to keep your sanity when you sleep on the hard frozen concrete of the city jungle. So now I will let you decide. What's worse? Having to find ways to wake up early and work on your dreams no matter how hard or being homeless? I think I will let common sense answer this question.

Coming back to our to-do lists, which are meant to keep us motivated, I discovered that it is essential to acknowledge how you have been spending your time and energy on things that don't matter so much. Instead of doing twenty or thirty tasks per day, with very little outcome, our energy depleted as a result, it's imperative that we set priorities, we choose clear goals. Let's say we have set our to-do list for next week. We will look over it and see which thing requires more energy to be achieved, as it will also be the one to bring the highest satisfaction.

Choose three to five priorities for that week to start with. Do this on Monday, first thing in the morning, because once you've achieved what was the hardest, the rest will take care of itself. Pick out five things to do that week. Then, look at your list and choose the one that makes you feel uncomfortable. Label them as 1, 2, 3, 4, and 5, according to the corresponding level of difficulty. In doing so, you will save a lot of energy, becoming proficient at time management. Remember, the key is to be productive, not just active. If you have completed all the major tasks, the most difficult ones, then even if you get a cold or come down with the flu, you can still do the remaining tasks, as they don't require that much energy or might not matter as much.

Les Brown, motivational speaker, once said: "If you do what is easy, then your life will be hard. But if you do what is hard, then your life will be easy". You can apply this dictate to all the areas of your life.

"If you can't fly, then run. If you can't run, then walk. If you can't walk, then crawl. But whatever you do, you must keep on moving forward." (Martin Luther King Jr.)

CHAPTER 8

THE ABC OF FINANCIAL AWARENESS

"Money is a source of energy, which only amplifies who you are as a person. So please strive to be good because money will eventually come." (Unknown)

First, what is financial awareness? It means that one can take financial decisions and manage finances to benefit your investments in the long term. This should lead to financial freedom, a concept every millennial uses nowadays. What does it mean? It can mean different things to different people, but I usually think of it as never having to worry about food, bills, or having a roof over your head.

To become independent or free from a financial point of view, there are certain steps you will have to follow.

1. Visualise your goals. Think about how much you want to achieve them, how long they will take, and how you want to make them come true.

It is essential to find a healthy balance in the present. What do I mean by that? Do not let greed guide your visualisations. It doesn't make sense to want a billion pounds within a year unless you're running a billion-euro company. At the same time, do not limit yourself. If you want to have and make millions, that's fine, but try to identify the amount that makes you happy and not the one advertised on mass media. Trust me when I say that you don't need millions to be happy. I'm not saying that such a sum won't make you happy. The truth is that there are plenty of people who happy, as they are earning ten thousand pounds per month, and they live their dream life.

Go into a deep visualisation meditation, a guided one if necessary, and start imagining what would it feel like to have that amount of money. Picture yourself buying the things that you've always wanted, strolling on sandy beaches, hiking in the coldest mountains, skydiving, flying private planes, or going on retreats, whatever you want. Close your eyes, take ten deep breaths, and relax your mind and body. Sit up with your back straight or lie down, if you are comfortable, this is all that matters.

You can do this by imagining that you have a *mind palace* in your head, where you can access your land of financial freedom. All you must do is to open the door of your superconscious highway. In that land, you can do whatever you desire. You have your personal virtual reality, which is connected to the highest source of energy. There, you can play with your financial imagination however you like, because there is an unlimited abundance that flows through your channels of energy and consciousness.

Think and visualise the monthly amount that would make you happy and content. Visualise that you have it, imagine how you are holding it. Give yourself time to achieve this goal, don't be afraid and try to be as realistic as possible. Then imagine how would you earn this amount, what new skills you must develop, what kind of personal development you must invest in, to increase your income and then get to work. Allow time to work its magic and be patient. If you put in the work, you will attain your goals, even if they might not happen when you wanted to. Always remember to never spend your money before you have them.

2. Make a vision board.

This is super important. A vision board can help you recondition your subconscious mind and its beliefs. The more you see it, the easier it can become your reality. Set up a nice big board, adding photographs of the things you want, whether it's a car, a house, or five of each. Do not limit yourself, but always remember that what you stick on the board should be your reality, and not the one seen on adverts. Those aren't really your dreams, that is something most people fail to understand. They have a friend who has a Ferrari, and they want one too. Or they've watched too many adverts, having the false impression certain things will make them happy.

You must dive deep to find your true happiness. Maybe a 4x4 car would be what you need and would make you happy. But because you lack the necessary clarity, you will end up working towards the wrong dream, owning a car that doesn't suits your needs. Let's say that you want to be a kickboxer or a boxer. Put up a picture with one or a few of your favourite fighters in the world like Muhamad Ali or Mike Tyson. Your vision board should include between five to ten goals that you would like to achieve. In addition, you should always be able to upgrade it, however you feel like.

It should include what you would like to achieve, financially, emotionally, relationship wise, business, or personal artistic dreams, a family, a house, a satisfactory state of health, cars, boats. Let your imagination flow freely. If you have your main desk, where you work every day, put it up there on the wall. Or you can put it wherever you spend most of your time. Make it as bright, big, and colourful as possible. To ensure it lasts longer, you can laminate or even frame it. It is essential that your brain sees it several times a day.

If you have a specific passion, like playing the violin, put a few photographs and some of your favourite quotes up. You can place them around the house, even in your car, at your work office or business place. Do not be shy or limited, and do not care about what people will think about it, because the naysayers and non-believers are not part of your journey. They don't know your struggle, and how much work you are putting in every day. For them, your goals are most likely unachievable, because they are lazy and have a limited mind. Detach yourself from them and stay focused, your path is yours and yours alone.

I remember the first time I made a vision board. I was about twenty-five years old and trust me when I say that I made it very flashy. I put down two houses, one up in the mountains and one by the sea, a Rolls Royce, and ten million euros. Then, I laminated and framed it, I added paper bills, each one of one million, and put them in a circle, so that it would resemble the sun.

Friends came into my home and called me crazy upon seeing the vision board. They kept asking me how I was going to achieve my goals and I would usually respond "with hard work and discipline". To be fair, seven years ago, I didn't really knew exactly how I would make it, but I stayed consistent. I kept reading books, taking courses, attending seminars and online courses, and I took care of my health, as best as I could.

Maybe half of those dreams weren't even mine. To be honest, most of them came from what I had seen in movies and on Instagram. Seven years later, I have gained more clarity. With hard work and discipline and waking up at 4 in the morning, I have fulfilled most of my dreams. I have a house by the sea and two cars. I haven't got those millions, as I understood that wasn't necessarily my wish. And I am content with making five thousand pounds a month for now and striving for ten over time. Right now, I am focused on my emotional balance, family, health, and business. My goals have changed and so will yours.

3. Start working on your mindset.

I would advise anyone to take at least one financial course and read books on how to make and manage money. Because such things are not taught at school. Just think about it. How else are the rulers of the world going to develop the first-world countries, if not with builders, carpenters, health workers, food industry workers, mechanics, electricians, accountants from third-world countries. These people travel the world, hoping to make a better life for themselves, whilst dealing with racism and discrimination daily, being overworked and underpaid at the same time. Nobody talks about this, and if they do, they are shut down with ease. I mention this issue, should it resonate with you, and so that you can understand that you are not alone. Millions of people have fallen into this trap, including myself.

Getting back to your mindset, it is essential to understand what money mean to you, what they represent, and how you perceive them. Money represents a source of energy, who amplify who you are as a person. Most people were raised with the belief that having money is bad, and they attached many negative connotations to this status. However, this is not the case, and for you to change that mentality, you must make an active effort.

Whenever you find yourself being judgemental towards somebody who has more money than you, reverse that mindset. Consider how they have worked for their wealth, or even if they haven't, it's not their fault that you feel this way. Try to become friends instead of judging them, and you will open a new pathway, where they will probably teach you how to make more money. You can also copy their healthy behaviours.

I want to give you a quick assignment. Go online and buy some movie money, you know, the fake kind. Then, put them wherever you spend most of your time. Put some in your car, in your backpack or purse, next to your vision board.

Truth be told, I have a very good reason for which I am asking you to do this. You are probably familiar with the saying "fake it until you make it". Well, this is only half true; to see your dreams come true, you must also put in the work. However, when you place those money around the house or visualise using them as payment, your subconscious mind can't tell the difference between what is fake and what is real. It is just like when you are watching a scary movie at the cinema and you get scared, even though you know no one is going to hurt you. You still get scared, and your body moves in your seat, because the subconscious mind can't tell the difference.

Therefore, having that money around you will help your mind create new neurological pathways for abundance. You will be able to change your mindset, finally understanding that you always have enough, sometimes more than you need. You can play with them, feel them, smell them, imagine that you are paying your bills, buying your dream car, or going on holiday. You are training the mind and shifting your perception. Carrying a stack of cash all the time will strengthen your confidence.

You are worthy and deserving of everything you desire. In exchange, you will attract people and experiences to benefit your financial journey. Naysayers have no place in your life. Even if you might find yourself on a lonely journey, a hard one, know that it will all be worth it, because your financial freedom is not just financial freedom. When you have money, life becomes easier. If you are going through hardship and you are in pain, isn't it better to only worry about how to overcome that emotional hardship, than having to worry about paying the bills as well?

4. Start working on your dream.

You might not see your dreams come true, if you only sit around, hoping that your visualisations will become real. The law of attraction is not enough, and neither is the concept of "fake it until you make it". You should not hope for your God to fill your bag either. I will give you a house building example, which can be applied to any other areas of your life, if you can just extract the main idea out of it.

Imagine you want a house. You will begin to draw it, make a plan, only to sit back and have a cup of tea, waiting for the house to appear on its own. God and your belief in the universal law of attraction are essential to see your dream come true, but the last time I checked, nobody will come to do your work for you. No one will come to dig your hole, raise your foundation, build your walls, fit your roof, etc.

It is up to you to handle all that, or you can hire somebody to do it. Think about the law of percentages. The work you put in matters; it will establish how much you will gain from it. Imagine you put in fifty percent of your energy into building a house. That is okay, but the outcome is going to be exactly as much as you put in. This is entirely up to you.

Believing in Gods and in the universal laws will help along the way. Let's say you want to find an electrician for your house. Just thinking of one is not going to help. You need to do your research and make a couple of phone calls. Maybe ask friends and family for recommendations or call in a few electricians for estimates. Then, the law of attraction will come into play, sending you the right person. A specialist who will resonate with your needs. You will come to an agreement regarding the price, and you will benefit from an excellent job, because the universe sees that you mean business and that kind of commitment deserves respect. In addition, you will establish a new relationship, from which you will stand a lot to gain. During the project, the electrician might introduce you to a good plumber or decorator. Whatever the case might be, you are creating new pathways through the work that you have put in, as always.

It is essential to have faith. While you are working on your dreams, things might go wrong. People will get sick or hurt, they might be in accidents, and their suffering will affect you. They are part of life, such things happen often, everywhere around the world. Events like this are to be expected and you need to take these occurrences into account, as this will make your journey easier. When faced with failure, remember to adopt a positive mindset. They are part of the growth process.

5. Keep working and never give up.

I might repeat myself, but this comes from a good place, as I know how easily people give up nowadays. My purpose is to motivate you, so that you can do the same for others. No matter how hard life gets, you should never give up. Giving up becomes an unhealthy habit, one which is hard to get rid of. The more you indulge in this habit, abandoning the things you enjoy, the harder it will be to get back to them. Failing is all right, quitting is not, in fact it is unacceptable. One should try to fail as many times as possible, because that is proof you have tried, proof you have never given up. And this is one of the best habits you can integrate in your life.

Humans are born with this strength of never giving up. Throughout history, it lessened. The educational systems are at fault, not to mention the professional aspect of life. I am talking about the jobs where one is selling their time and health for a few pennies, their self-worth being trampled upon, until it exists no more. I can understand how hard it is to overcome that conditioning. That's why we must re-educate ourselves.

Did you know that babies learn to crawl first, from six to nine months. They are strengthening their muscles in preparation for the next milestone. Crawling is practiced daily. Then, they will need between six months and a year to take their first steps and start walking. For the next couples of years, they would have fallen down hundreds of times, until they learn how to walk.

Imagine if we had all given up on walking, abandoning the learning process. Instead, we learned from our mistakes. Fair enough, we had our parents to support us. Nevertheless, we can tap into that attitude again, choosing to persevere. We can look at those falls as our learning failures and surround yourself with people who care about us. People who support us, who are there for us, in good and in difficult times. Maybe your parents aren't present in your life anymore or they don't resonate with your dream. As soon as you grow up and become independent, if you don't have a supporting family, you must create one for yourself, whether it's through relationships, friendships, or marriage. Remember to stay focused, to never give up. Always get up after a fall, dust yourself, and get back on the horse. You deserve to see your dreams come true, and you owe it to yourself to become the greatest version possible.

6. Enjoy the fruits of your hard labour.

After all the hard work and years of personal development, after having to go through the fires of hell at times, the time has come for you to enjoy your achievements. It's time for you to rest and take the holidays you dreamed of. Maybe buy something you've always wanted or visit the seven wonders of the modern world if such things are part of your dreams. Remember to maintain a healthy balance. Do not become so involved in your work that you forget to take a break or spend time with your family. Set time aside for yourself as well. Do not give into greed. When you achieve your financial goals, refrain from spending all your money, buying various things, which let's be honest, are not necessarily needed. Be aware of your actions all the time. After all those years of commitment, I am sure you have developed your self-awareness and self-control. As a result, you can lead a happy and balanced life. If you stay focused and follow these simple adaptable steps for your financial journey, nothing can stop you from achieving your money goals.

I was born in a family that was poor and broken. I used to eat biscuits from the ground, when I would find them on the playground, left by the other kids, because I was hungry and didn't always have food. As a result, I grew up with the limited mentality that being poor but happy is all right, which by the way is wrong. That saying has no value and it should have no place in our minds. I've always wanted what I never had or what I saw at the rich kids around me, toys, clothing, fancy foods, bikes, cars, and so on. But I knew that my life isn't going to change unless I do. So, I had to change my mentality on money and take responsibility for my own actions, daring to have bigger dreams and follow through. To succeed, first we must work on changing our belief system. To make money, you must follow the ABC of financial awareness, step by step, and commit to it like your life depends on it. At least seventy percent of your life is influenced by it, that is the truth.

For more clarity, I recommend you try these two steps as well.

Step one

There are two easy steps to follow. Let's say you are broke and in debt, without a home to live in. That's the lowest you can be from a financial point of view, stuck in survival mode. If you have nothing, get over your pride and search for a job. It does not matter what kind of job, if you are accepted. You should then work as hard as you can, take several jobs, if necessary, until you would have made enough to pay your bills and your debt.

Try to save at least 30% of your income, whether we are talking about a weekly or monthly income. Do not forget to repay your debt first. If you want to make money, you must have money. There is no other way around it, there are no shortcuts. This is the golden rule, unless you're going to do illegal things and we all know that is not going to work on a long-term basis, it is not sustainable.

Always remember to pay yourself first. If you are getting paid two thousand pounds per month, you first pay yourself the 30%, because you're the most important person in your life. Once you have saved a few thousand pounds and you can finally get out of the house, you can invest in your chosen automated business. But before you are going to make money, we need to make sure that you have changed your mentality. Otherwise, you won't know how to spend or invest them, and you'll end up like one of those people who have won the lottery. They ended up with a colossal amount of money and didn't know how to manage it. Therefore, they lost it within a year or less, and they were broke again.

You should have at least five sources of income. Number one pays the bills. Number two is a separate income that you should never touch, unless it's a life-or-death type of situation. Number three covers your own expenses. Number four is for you to travel and enjoy life, don't abuse it, but try to enjoy it. And number five allows you to save money and invest in yourself. You can use it for personal development, to learn new skills or take an online course. All these things will help you to make more money. If you start managing your money like this, even if you do not have too much, you will always act with abundancy in mind, certain that you always have enough.

Step two

The second step involves changing your limiting beliefs and old patterns that have kept you poor. To do that, you must know yourself, and most importantly the ideas you associate with money. Do you believe, just like I did in the past, that money is the root of all evil, that being broke but happy is all right, or that rich people are mean people? Let me tell you something. Rich people aren't bad because of the money they have, well maybe some of them are, but not all of them. The point is that money doesn't make you good or bad.

Money represents a positive source of energy, something that amplifies who you are as a person. If you're a criminal, but you have money, guess what, you'll be a criminal with a lot of money. You are going to cause harm much easier, as you can acquire weapons with ease and whatever else such a person would buy. If you're a good person and earn more money, guess what, that will help you become a much better person or a philanthrope, someone who travels around the world and helps this planet become a better place.

Now I will show you how to change your old patterns. Look at the last five years of your life and how much money you had at the end of each year. Did you manage to save any? If not, check your spending, were you buying things just because you wanted them? My thought process is like this. If you're broke, you should only buy the things you need, not the ones you want. It is as simple as that. You know what needs to change. Check your winnings as well see, to identify a potential pattern. Take a pen and a piece of paper and note everything that seems important and needs to change. Only you know the truth, your own truth.

I knew a young guy who checked his financial pattern for the last five years. Each year, he used to make a nice sum of money for his age. Then, he would just waste it on buying things that were useless. He would earn five to ten thousand, two or three times per year, and then he would spend the money within a couple of weeks maximum. And I am talking about hard earned money, as he was working overtime on construction sites. Who was that guy? My younger self.

I worked hard to notice and understand my financial pattern. Then, I changed it by being conscious of my earnings and spendings. If you are aware of these things, it's much easier to make a financial plan for the next couple of years. Always remember to manage your money when you are poor. Such habits will help you stay on track with your spendings. Make a list with all your bills and spendings; and remember to save until you have enough to invest. When you feel like spending money on things that you don't need, you are harming your financial freedom. The more you do it, the more you postpone your freedom. And you know what they say about postponing. The more you do it, the more difficult your future is going to be. You're not getting any younger, and even if you're only in your twenties, do not underestimate the value of money management.

Once you have enough money to invest, make sure that you don't keep all your eggs in one basket. That's the golden rule of being rich. Start working on creating at least five sources of passive income. One to pay your bills, one to pay your expenses (food, clothing, etc.), one for the savings account, one to invest in your growth, and one to enjoy life, including for travels and hobbies, like playing the violin or guitar, etc. How can you create these sources if you're absolutely broke?

Find work even if it is paid almost nothing. There is only one way up the financial ladder. If you want to make money, you must keep going, no matter how hard it is. Just please try not to diminish your spirit along the way and keep your integrity intact. Once you made some money and you have a place to live, try to invest your money into an automatization style or passive source of income. Maybe invest in a business, find an online job, pursue a passion, or try network marketing. Other options include crafts for talented persons, Forex automated software, book writing, or IT program development. This list can be incredibly long, so I'll just stop here. I hope that you got the picture.

Remember to do a thorough research before making investments. Working on your dream can be rewarding both emotionally and financially. You can see your dreams come through with commitment and consistency. However, if a business doesn't work, don't quit, or give up on it. Just because it's hard, it doesn't mean you are failing. Maybe you need to learn more about it. Take some courses, you have money saved and you can use them for such purposes.

Once you have your five sources of income, you might feel comfortable enough to move to the next level. You can quit your job if you hate it, most people are dealing with a similar situation. If you love your job and it fulfils you, then it is perfectly okay to keep it. But if that's not the case, you can finally start working on your dreams and follow your passion. A mediocre life is not worth living. What is more, we all have a purpose on this planet. Money gives you freedom, so that it becomes easier to overcome life's challenges.

Everyone should have big dreams, including yourself. You can start working towards financial abundance, so that you can travel wherever you want and whenever you want, assuming that is your dream. You can automate your investments and businesses, benefitting from financial abundance. As a result, your wealth will create more joy in the world for you and for others. This financial balance will also guarantee a secure future, not just for yourself, but for your loved ones as well.

Financial abundancy equals a worry-free life for yourself and your family. It will benefit your kids and most probably your grandkids, especially if you are planning to leave something behind. This is worth considering. If you haven't thought about it until now, be sure to put it on your list. Think of what you would want to leave behind. Your legacy should be the thing for which you wake up excited in the morning, the things that offer or bring you a sense of fulfilment. Choose things that will help this world become better and think of them as your contribution to the world that will continue to exist after you are gone.

Write them down on a piece of paper or print them out. You can then post them near your bed, so they are the first thing you see when you wake up, very much like an alarm clock if that can be said. It is essential to invest in your legacy, especially if you want to improve this world for future generations. Such actions will help you find fulfilment and true happiness in life, so remember to invest in yourself. As a result, you will become the greatest version of yourself, helping your family, friends, and your community. I am certain that everyone wants to do good, it's just a matter of resources. You must have money to make money, there are rarely other ways. The key is to be patient, especially if you are working on your long-term dream.

"If it is a necessity, buy it. If it is a wanting desire, postpone it, create self-control."

CHAPTER 9

OPPORTUNITIES VS ACTION TAKING

"Opportunities are usually disguised as hard work, so most people don't recognize them." (Ann Landers)

We live in one of the most advanced eras, where information is easily accessible. We have voice controls, thanks to the innovative AI, with technology evolving at a rapid pace. If there is anything you ever dreamed of doing or becoming, you can get an online mentor or watch videos on how to do it step by step. Whether you are just beginning or have a degree of experience, there are options to educate yourself. This is an absolute amazing opportunity; you can see your dreams come true without having to invest ample amounts of money. Just act and see where you will arrive at. A smartphone is enough in the beginning, as it will allow you to work towards your dreams. Opportunity and action work together. And there might be a million opportunities coming your way, but if you don't act, they will turn out to be worthless.

So, what is an opportunity? It represents a favourable or advantageous circumstance that presents to someone, allowing them to take action and achieve a particular goal or outcome. It can show up in various forms, such as a new job, a chance to learn something new, a business partnership, or a personal relationship. An opportunity can enhance one's life or different experiences in one way or another.

Just like Ann Landers says, it often requires some effort or hard work. Sometimes, it might even be necessary to take risks. Recognizing and seizing opportunities can be a crucial factor in achieving success in many areas of life.

Sometimes, we notice how people got lucky or had an opportunity for their business. The truth is that these didn't just came out of nowhere. That person dreamed of such things or made a minimum of effort, writing his or her dreams on a piece of paper. Most of them have worked hard for a particular situation to happen.

Here is an example. When I was about twenty-five years old, I used to work on a building site as a labourer, and I was fired because they didn't needed help anymore. So here I was, looking for another job. At the time, I was working hard on my personal development. Wherever i was working, that would reflect in my workspace. I wanted to become a site supervisor, so I was doing my courses and looking for jobs. Unfortunately, I had to pay rent, so I took the first job that I found, working as a labourer again.

Two days into my new job, the manager of the construction site left his job for personal reasons. I heard what happened and I was naturally interested in being given his job. And so, I've started to cleverly work my way up there. I decided to rearrange the materials and tools on the construction site. One of the managers saw me and he realized that I was an excellent professional. The storage facility had been left in a complete mess. He asked me if I wanted to work as a store manager and I said yes. The opportunity presented itself and I did not hesitate to take immediate action.

Opportunities will come your way, but if you do not act, someone else will benefit from them. That person might have similar goals or dreams. In my situation, it all started with a desire, as I wanted to become a site supervisor. I then took the necessary action, learning the skills for the job. In the end, I accepted the manager position. The universe is willing to give to those who ask. But it will all depend on how much work are you willing to put in. Nothing will come your way unless you manifest your intentions or desires.

Hard work and discipline will bring plenty of opportunities in your lifetime. And if you pay close attention, you will catch those that will benefit you. Sometimes, it may take longer than you expected. You might think that your shot will not appear. I encourage you to remember the bamboo tree and how it takes up to five years to come out of the ground. In the beginning, it only has a couple of centimetres. Then it will grow at an amazing speed within a short period of time. This is why we must practise patience. Like we spoke in the previous chapter, patience is a virtue, a long-term goal that will benefit you. Just be patient and pay attention. Do not be afraid to think about what you desire. Dream of them as often as possible.

Do not let an opportunity pass by, because you might not get another one of this kind or someone else could get it before you. In the wild, when the lions hunt, they usually choose the weakest from the herd. This is so that they can catch it fast, with the least amount of energy spent. Sometimes, the respective herd does not have a wounded or weak animal, such as a zebra or antelope. A hungry lion will attack the first animal in its path with strong decisiveness. It will go straight for the jugular. That is how you must behave in our concrete jungle. Whether you are talking about your business or personal life experiences, act like a lion. Do not wait for an easier opportunity to come your way. Accept that you might feel uncomfortable, take what's yours and what you deserve.

Let me tell you a story that holds a valuable lesson within.

A young man wanted to marry the daughter of a farmer, who was very beautiful. He went to her father and asked for his permission to marry his daughter. The farmer looked at him and said, "I will allow you to marry my daughter, but you have to fulfil one condition". He then told him, "Go out and stand in the field. I am going to release three bulls, one at a time, and you must grab their tail. If you can catch the tail of any bull, then you can marry my daughter". And so, the young man went to the designated field and stood there, waiting for bulls to be released.

The barn door opened and out came one of the biggest bulls he had ever seen. He decided to let that one go and wait for the second bull. He stepped aside and let the bull pass. The barn opened and out came the second bull. This one was bigger and fiercer than the previous bull. The boy thought that maybe the next one could be a better choice, so he ran to the side and let the bull pass through.

The door opened for the third time and out came the last bull. The boy had a big smile on his face. The last bull was the weakest he had ever seen. He positioned himself, ready to take on the bull and grab his tail. As the bull ran towards him, he waited for the right moment to complete his mission. To his surprise, the third bull had no tail.

The morale of the story is obvious. Life is full of opportunities, but if we miss the first one, just because we waited for something better, we might end up with nothing. This is an inspiring story and I think we should all apply it in our lives, regardless of how old we are. As a young person, you might think that you have all the time in the world. Undoubtedly, you have more time than an older person. But remember that time doesn't buy opportunities, nor does it create them. So, seize your moment and grab your opportunity even if it feels uncomfortable. Whatever makes you feel uncomfortable today, will make you stronger and wiser tomorrow. Only through action you can experience life and what it has to offer.

Brian Tracy has an amazing book, called "Eat that Frog", which holds a lot of valuable lessons. His recommendation is to always take care of the thing that makes you feel insecure or uncomfortable. Then, you will be able to take care of the easy ones, without too much difficulty. The same lesson can be applied to opportunities. You should grab one when it appears and use it to your advantage. It might not save your life at that moment, but I can assure you that it will help you along the way, on your life path, offering a lesson that you'll never forget.

In my case, that experience helped me understand that if I kept acting, grabbing the opportunities coming my way, I will benefit forever. We don't want to grow old and spend the rest of our time regretting the things we haven't tried, because we were afraid. Afraid of what might people think, or maybe we were too shy. Perhaps we were afraid to take a risk that could've changed our life for the better. We didn't approach a girl we liked because we were too shy or missed a business opportunity because we were too afraid to take a chance.

I heard many stories about people who led a miserable existence as a couple, living in the same house and under the same roof for over twenty years, without loving each other. A mundane and painful way of living, with comfort chosen over freedom. You must allow yourself to be free, especially in this society, where life already feels like a prison itself. People shouldn't choose to stay together, just because they are afraid of what their family or friends will think of them. They shouldn't give into old religious beliefs, considering it is a sin to divorce.

How can it be a sin to divorce, when you have tried everything to fix up your relationship, but nothing seems to work? There is only this much we can do to improve our relationship. We might try to change ourselves, but we can't expect others to change for us, that is a sin. It is essential to get rid of old beliefs. God loves you, and if God loves you, do you think that He would want you to live miserably for so many years? He doesn't want to see you living in pain, leading a life of quiet desperation, where you know that freedom is what you want and need. In such cases, divorce is the best option. People can then go on their separate ways. If you find yourself in this same situation, keep in mind that new paths and new people will come your way, because you deserve to be loved and to be free.

I know a man who gave up in his fifties, which let's be honest, is not the same as when you are in your thirties, but it's not an old age either. You can still move mountains, as fifty is the age of maturity, when you still have the energy to start a new life or a new career, to find a spouse or somebody to spend your life with. That man has been through two marriages, and he has four kids. They are all grown-ups and have their own families. His last wife left without a trace, after sixteen years of marriage. He did not have the chance to divorce, and he never thought of looking for her either.

As I am writing this book, twenty years after these events, he is about seventy-three and his biggest regret is that he doesn't have a house, a roof over his head. This person is my dad, and for the last twenty years he has been living as a victim. Alcohol took control over his life, causing him to become an alcoholic. He has been living at the mercy of his kids, who have made sure he has money and a roof under his head. Unfortunately, he has turned into an ungrateful alcoholic, someone who has never appreciated the help given to him. He now lives in a mental prison, and he is full of regrets and sorrows, especially about past mistakes.

He has been drinking his entire life. Now he is retired, and he has even more time to drink. My dad lives in a rental, regretting the fact that he never bought a house. Looking at the positive side of this experience has helped. I was raised by an alcoholic father and my mother was absent, so I promised to myself that I would repeat their mistakes. In my youth, as well as my late twenties, I was on a similar path, maybe even worse. Sometimes we must repeat the same mistake at least ten times to learn the lesson. So here I am, trying to become the best version of myself, despite my traumatic past.

In the past twenty years, my dad had many opportunities to find a job, to connect with new people, but where there is no will, there is no desire. This lack of ambition can cause us to miss out on all the opportunities coming our way. Life might hit you hard, trust me it will, and you might end up on a dark path. That is all right, as long as you won't let it take your entire power away. You can cry to release your suffering, and you might even start drinking if you don't have other healthy coping mechanisms. My advice would be to not spend more than six months or a year in this situation. Try to find your way out of the darkness and if you are willing to change, new opportunities will come your way. Remember that you owe it to yourself to become your greatest version in this lifetime. And even if it's not an easy journey, it is much better than ending up old, without a roof under your head and full of regrets. Instead of leading a peaceful existence, you might struggle with medical afflictions caused by impoverishment, addicted to substances that will crush your spirit and willpower.

CHAPTER 10

VIRTUES, RESPECT AND VALUES

"The true measure of a man is not how he behaves in moments of comfort and convenience, but how he stands at times of controversy and challenges." (Martin Luther King Jr.)

Virtues

Thousands of years ago, long before democracy was invented, some of the greatest philosophers of that time, such as the great Marcus Aurelius, Aristotle, Plato, and Socrates, were led their existence according to the most vital and reliable virtues of life. Aristotle, the Greek philosopher, was the one to identify the eleven virtues of life, virtues which everyone should aspire to. Let us dive into this a little deeper, so as to understand which values, we should tap into the most, and which are the ones we can pursue for our personal wisdom.

<u>The eleven virtues of life</u>

1. Courage
2. Temperance
3. Liberality

4. Magnificence
5. Magnanimity
6. Patience
7. Truthfulness
8. Wittiness
9. Friendliness
10. Justice
11. Modesty

I will be breaking them down in a modern way, because not everyone can understand the old way of the philosophers.

Courage

What does it mean to be courageous? The answer is quite simple. It means to be able to do something that others are afraid of. Courage represents a mental strength, with people having the determination to venture and withstand diverse fears, or to try something that is difficult. We all need to be more courageous in the different aspects of our lives. Courage can mean talking to a girl you like as a teenager, opening your mind and heart so that you can heal from a traumatic experience, or asking your boss about the raise you deserve.

Courage is not a given, unless you have been brought up in a healthy environment, with a normal amount of self-esteem. Most people, however, grew up hearing phrases like 'you are not going to amount to anything' or 'you are a worthless piece of shit', usually from their parents. For others, the situation was even worse. They only had a parent or had to grow up without parents. As a result, they lacked a mentor, that person who is supposed to guide you in life. If you are one of those people, then you should read the chapter on unconditional love. This will help you gain the courage to love yourself, as well as to stop caring about what others think of you.

You must be careful with this virtue of life because it is just like a coin. It has two sides, and you must find a way to "hold" it, so that you can see both sides. Do not allow it to be tilted to one of the sides, otherwise you will lose your balance. I grew up just with my father and as a boy was, I only saw one side of the coin. I wasn't afraid of trying new things. Truth be told, I was the first to jump from up high or climb the highest tree in the forest or at the park. I used to get into fights as well.

I could not see the other side of the coin, it was missing. So, I didn't know how to talk to a girl. I was shy and I didn't know how to start a conversation. And I kept thinking that I was not good enough, which hurt my self-esteem. I never had the chance to be balanced and courageous in my youth. You must be careful in life, because excess courage can cause you to become selfish, which in turn will lead you on a slippery road. This might cause you to take harsh decisions, which will harm you and those around you. Driving drunk is just one of the many examples I can give you.

Let's take another hypothetical situation. Imagine you are with your friends on a safari trip. As you are touring the jungle in a jeep, you decide to take a closer selfie with a rhino or a lion, despite the fact you have been instructed by the tour guides and everyone else to stay in the car for the entire tour duration. And guess what, that lion wasn't in the mood for that courageous bullshit, so typical for a white person. Your arm has been bitten off, and you have endangered the others as well, by waking up the whole pack of lions. Next thing you know, you live the rest of your life with one arm, just because you had to prove yourself, or even worse to people who maybe don't care about you. You did something stupid, which maybe at the time you mistook for courage.

Being an adrenaline junkie has never been the way to heal fear. Maybe it could work when it comes to the fear of heights or jumping, but it doesn't make you invincible, at least not in a conscious way. And you must remember the other side of the coin. You must be courageous and jump when an opportunity arises, otherwise you will end up thinking that you are a coward. Years later, you will regret not talking to that girl or asking for the desired raise. Ultimately, what I am saying is you should have enough courage to persevere in life. Just don't let your ego do the driving, as you might end up making the wrong choices.

Temperance

Self-care is a grand virtue. You are making a conscious choice to not harm your body, avoiding both drugs and alcohol. I will talk about this topic in depth, because it represents something we all encounter, teenagers. Stimulating substances and alcohol have a harming effect, affecting people all around the world. The effect is not just physical but mental and emotional. Alcohol is responsible for the deaths of around two hundred thousand people in Europe only, because it causes liver disease and cancer, and it is responsible for severe accidents. It represents the third biggest cause of early death and illness in Europe, after smoking and high blood pressure.

Alcohol is responsible for the broken families, where husbands beat their wives, who are then violent towards the children. This represents a harmful and vicious circle. There is a very good reason for which alcohol is cheap and easy to get, even though it should be illegal because of its effect over people. Alcohol is part of a huge industry, which won't kneel easily, for its own selfish reasons. It does not matter for how many deaths and broken families alcohol is responsible.

When nothing else can be done, it is essential for one to seek a healthy balance in life. Teenagers often start drinking from a young age and become addicted, as they lack a proper education. It is easy for them to start drinking, even if they don't like it at first. They might want to seem tougher than they are, with alcohol giving them the courage they need to talk to a girl or get into a fight. I know how they feel, as I was in the same situation as a teenager, becoming an addict with the passing of time.

You shouldn't allow addiction to go on, given its harmful effects. Most people manage to break free from their addiction only when they mature and have responsibilities. It is only then that they understand how harmful it is. Some might need longer to get to that point. In the end, you must give up alcohol, otherwise you will wake up years later, feeling sorry for yourself. By then, alcohol most likely turned you into a victim.

Alcohol abuse is the equivalent of spiritual suicide. Nothing good comes from this addiction. If you think that alcohol abuse has a beneficial side, then you are lying to yourself, as I did for years. You might drink alcohol just because you don't know how to cope without it in certain situations. But I can assure you that you can face anything, you can get over any situation, no matter how bad it might be.

Begin by admitting that you are an addict and here I am not talking about alcohol only. If you are dealing with addiction, acknowledge its presence and find a way to break free. Use your conscious awareness and free will, otherwise you will return to the same place, until you will eventually lose control of your life. Maybe you're the kind who has a glass of wine once a month or even less than that. Please try to drink quality wine, from someone who makes it from their own vineyard.

I don't encourage alcohol consumption at all, due to my past experiences. As a former addict, I can tell you that addiction has led to me losing friends and family, having money issues, and fighting with low self-esteem. Now I understand the devastating effect of addiction and how it could make me lose the control over my own life. When it comes to abstinence, I believe that one should practice it throughout his or her entire life, religiously so to speak. As a result, it will come more easily and naturally.

Liberality

Generosity is amazing, and I am not talking just about philanthropy, because not everyone can afford to give away millions to those in need. You don't need money to be kind, we all have a heart. It is not necessary to become Mother Teresa either. Indeed, she was a saint, and her story is amazing. You can help others with money, but you can also be considerate and empathic. When an old person talks to you, whether that person is someone you love, like your parent, or a stranger, please listen to them. Don't just half-listen, give them the respect and the help needed, because they can be just as needy as little kids. They won't say it, because they might be shy or don't want to think of themselves as worthless. Help your neighbours when in need, become a part of the society that helps one way or another.

As I am writing this book, there is a war going on between Russia and Ukraine. The Russians have invaded Ukraine, nothing new there. Together with my wife, I have sent some money through the Red Cross, hoping that our donation will help those in need. We are also planning on hosting refugees in our house, as we are aware of the horrifying tragedies that a war can bring along, especially when looking back.

You must find a balance when it comes to helping others. Some people can be highly empathetic and prone towards helping others, reaching the point where they forget about themselves. That is not good, because if you can't help yourself, you might not be able to help others. To pull a drowning person out of a lake, first you must know how to swim. Otherwise, the both of you will drown. If you have more than you can carry, give some of it away. Refusing to do so, you will become burdened. Disease will follow. You should never be stingy, because we leave this world as we came, free of possessions. If you want to die at peace, it is best to have a light heart, free of selfishness and judgment.

Magnificence

Magnificence represents the virtue of spending generous amounts of money, to bring great things into this world, such as the Burj Khalifa, the Sistine Chapel, or the Great Wall of China. The list is long, and I bet there are many proud people out there, happy about whatever they have invested their time in. They use their fortune to build things all over the world, even if they needed an entire lifetime to see their dreams accomplished.

Not everything that has been built has a correct reasoning behind it, because a lot of things are created to feed the ego of rich people. Let me explain more about the virtue of magnificence and how to use it for the better of our planet. A good example is when someone builds something, like a bridge over a lake, so that people can travel from one side to another with ease. The ego comes into place when that lake is developed by a rich entity, which will then claim property rights, asking people to pay a certain fee for using the bridge. This is the opposite of magnificence.

Let's say that you decide to have a sculpture made. You can afford to make it grand, so you go ahead with your project. The intrinsic motivation for this project should be your community and the idea of the sculpture being enjoyed by everyone. If you do such a thing for your personal profit, then you are making a terrible mistake.

If your financial situation allows it, then you should pursue the virtue of magnificence. You will bring joy to the world, and that is the best motivation.
Thus, you will enjoy these things for the rest of your life, leaving something behind for future generations. A grand legacy, so that people always remember you and your accomplishments.

Magnanimity

The word magnanimity comes from the Latin *magnanimitas*, and it represents a calque of the Greek word *megalopsychia*, which means *great soul*. This term is used to describe the quality of having a great mind, heart, and spirit. Magnanimous people can rise above pettiness, are generous with their own emotions, and demonstrate the willingness to forgive when necessary. This is a grand virtue in many religions and cultures, and it is often associated with the idea of selflessness. Such people will often put the **needs of others before their own.**

Being kind and compassionate can help us access our higher self. This is beneficial for everyone, regardless of our life experiences. In the end, having a great soul can help you understand life and people much easier.

Patience

We all want to be more patient. Patience is a great quality, a true virtue. And, considering the times we are living in, it can be seen as a superpower. Imagine you are a teenager, and you can't wait to grow up. You want to be independent and have your own job, with your own money to spend. Most of us have been in that position, we wanted to grow up quickly and get away from our parents, maybe escape their constant punishment. Let's be honest, teenagers and patience don't mix well. When we are young, we want everything, right then and there.

Instead of a stressed teenager who can't wait to grow up, imagine if we would teach our kids to be patient. We can guide them to understand that some things cannot be changed by anything other than time. By adulthood, they would have developed this virtue, which will benefit not only them, but others as well. The importance of patience is clear. For instance, when we start a new business or learn a new skill, we need to be patient. Even if we want to achieve our goals fast, we must be patient and wait for them to happen in due time.

If we only knew from the beginning that we can't hurry things, as they happen naturally, if we are patient. That would save us from so much stress and unnecessary worries. Patience is your own superpower, do not hesitate to work on it.

Truthfulness

Being true to yourself will influence your relationship with others, in a good manner. This quality will help you stay on a straight path, one that is full of light. You probably heard this before, but those who tell the truth never have to lie. Now I'm not saying that I always say the truth, but if there is a percentage scale for it, I always aim for a minimum of 80%. Telling the truth is sometimes impossible, but my conscience is clear, as I only have innocent lies in my inventory.

It has never been easy to say what is on your mind, given the risk of hurting the feelings of those around you. For instance, you can't go to a five-year-old kid and tell him that Santa Claus doesn't exist. If you say such things, you will scar the poor child for life, taking some of his or her innocence away. That is the reason why most parents wait until their kids are older. In such situations, it's easier to tell a little white lie than the truth.

However, our society has been built on lies and superstitions. This was necessary to assert control over the masses, to influence the emotional wellbeing of the population. Unfortunately, we keep teaching the same things to future generations. Unless we are going to change our beliefs and habits, we will continue to have lies as part of human experience. Once you are ready to break through barriers and become free of society's requirements, you will be able to tap into the real side of truthfulness as a virtue.

Wittiness

Wittiness represents the ability to express yourself in a clever, amusing, and often ironic or unexpected way. It is a form of quick, intelligent humour that requires creativity, something stand-up comedians often possess. However, there is a big difference between making funny jokes and being sarcastic. You should never mistake racism for wittiness, and those who push negative agendas should never be associated with such qualities. We should acknowledge these things.

Let's take an example. Stand-up comedians make fun about different cultures, sexes, or minorities. They use humour to address issues of race, culture, and identity in a way that is intended to challenge stereotypes. In doing so, they bring people together. When such things are done right, it can promote understanding and empathy between humans.

Having this quality can be compared to having another extra life when you play a game online. Just like a little health bag that refills your life span. It can be used in our daily life as a healthy way of living. People who laugh more live more, so find ways to entertain yourself, even if you will end up laughing at your own jokes. That will extend your life path in a healthy manner. Learn how to laugh if you have to, learn sarcasm and irony, and ease your journey.

Friendliness

This might be the simplest of them all. We have all learned how to make friends as children, in some of the silliest ways. As a grown-up, we must keep those friendships alive and help each other in need. It might also help to praise each other, and to make room for different feelings, be it happiness or sadness. Being a true friend is great if there are healthy boundaries in place. A healthy evolving society is based on true friendships.

Let's compare the United States and Italy. You might go with any other Mediterranean country, but the conclusion would be the same. The people from these countries are friendly, not only between themselves but with others as well. Americans, on the other hand, call themselves united, but in truth they part of the most divided nation in the world. People are taught to become the best in most areas of life. You might see plenty of strong single mothers or powerful businessmen, people who made it without any help.

We don't need to be geniuses to understand how the power of many works. When you have the whole family working for the same goal, as opposed to just one person, it is clear who is going to evolve faster. Being a great friend will facilitate the positive emotional balance of an entire nation. A wall is always built wall by wall. Always remember this African proverb: "If you want to go fast, go alone, but if you want to go far, go together". You can decide which path to take. Just think of this proverb and your answer, and your life path will be revealed.

Justice

This is one of my favourites, since I have an injustice wound, which I had to learn how to overcome and heal in this lifetime. It is clear why it resonates with me the most.

Being just is a life virtue, but it might not be easy when it comes to applying it in real life. We can do that by asking ourselves a few simple questions. For instance, do we take action when we see that somebody might hit a little lady crossing the street? This is one example. Justice can mean different things to different people. However, I realized that we all have a common ground, on which our communities and societies are built. We cannot and we should not interfere with everything unless we want to take upon a godly burden. But whenever we see something that can be changed and it will benefit the world around us, we should act. We need to tap into our power, shifting the energies around us. Remember that we are born with willpower and a free will, both of which can be enhanced through real-life experiences. Try to be a just human being, someone who wants to help others, and make the world a better place.

Modesty

This is one of the hardest things to tap into nowadays since we can often hide our authentic selves behind the screen of a phone or a laptop. We might even hide behind our clothes or other materialistic things. Such actions can impede us from evolving because they keep us away from the outside world. A great lesson to learn here would be that no matter how rich you are or will become, you should never show off. Keep in mind that there are a lot of people who do not have a lot of money. Even if you perceive yourself to be more intelligent than your colleague or neighbour, do not let yourself be driven by the selfish high and mighty ego, as such things might also lead to an early, sad, and lonely grave. If you are rich, whether emotionally or financially, may you be blessed. In great wealth and wisdom, you have great responsibility towards yourself and the community that you live in. Try to practice modesty, as this will bring along people who will love and respect you.

With patience, over time, you will be able to develop some, if not all these virtues, thus benefitting from an easier lifetime experience. By practising these virtues to your very best, you will rediscover yourself as a new and reborn human being, with new and healthy superpowers that nobody can ever take them away from you. You can be stripped of clothes, money, and other materialistic things in this lifetime, but nobody can ever take your emotional intelligence and wisdom away. This is because you have acquired these through life experiences, hard work, and discipline. You can go through life without fear dominating because the energy and power that are within you cannot be broken, just like the human spirit. All that you have learned will transform you, and you will stand a lot to gain from these new superpowers.

"There is only one way to happiness, that is to cease worrying about things which are beyond the power of our will." (Epitectus)

CHAPTER 11

LEGACY

"I've learned that people will forget what you said, people will forget what you did, but people will never forget how you made them feel". (Maya Angelou)

     This is an essential chapter, not only in this book, but in your life as well. We need to consider what we will leave behind; think about the impact we will have on future generations. The bigger goal is the health of this planet that has taken care of us with kindness, allowing us to inhabit it without restraints. As a result, we have a responsibility not only to ourselves, but also to Mother Earth.

     What is a legacy? It usually refers to something that is handed down by previous generations, often in the form of tradition or inheritance. In a broader sense, it can also refer to the impact that a person or an organisation has on the world and the lasting impressions they leave behind. A legacy can be left in many ways, such as inventing something creative that helps society, or in the form of education. For instance, books represent common legacies. And here I am talking about books that had an impact on millions of people, books written by authors like Socrates, Fyodor Dostoevsky, William Shakespeare, etc. Or you can create courses, such as the ones that help people overcome their fear of public speaking, courses through which people learn how to heal themselves, in a natural or holistic way.

Anything that has an impact, with a positive influence over the world can be called a legacy. I know what some might say, and that is what about having kids, making babies. Well, that right there is a very controversial subject, and I have a very good reason for saying that. Legacy is something to be passed on, which means that it can take many different forms, such as one's faith, ethics, or belief systems. The main idea is to create a better future for the next generations.

Having kids is not something that requires a great intellectual effort, almost anyone who is healthy can become a parent. Reproduction is natural and a biological advantage. Children might be often perceived as legacies, but that is not true, because almost anyone can assume the role of parent. What matters is to be balanced from an emotional point of view, to have financial education and freedom, as this will help you raise and educate your children into well-adjusted human beings. That is the hard part.

It is only normal to be proud of your children and consider them your legacy. But if you think that the parents of Albert Einstein were responsible for what he became, you are wrong. They might have guided him on a particular path, but all the credit goes to himself. He was his own person, responsible for the choices he took, and the original source of all the creative ideas and inventions. He dealt with his emotional turmoil on his own.

Parents who see kids as their legacy on this planet have often failed to accomplish other things. They are trying to take some of the shine away from their kids, which is unfair. Their actions are connected to an old belief system, stemming from hundreds and hundreds of years ago, when having children was essential for the evolution of our species. As you can see nowadays, we are not on the verge of extinction, on the contrary. I do not believe in the idea of depopulation.

If you choose to have kids, you must assume responsibility for this decision. You need to give them financial security, because having a roof over your head is not enough. I know a guy who is in his forties, he has ten kids already. Whenever I ask him about it, he says that he is not going to stop. In his own words, if God gives him kids, he will have them. They all live in a single room with a kitchen next to it, in the countryside. The truth is that they live in the worst conditions possible. He is an alcoholic and the family is visited by the local authorities at least once a month, as the wife abuses the kids. I met some of the kids. The sixteen-year-old boy looks like he is nine and his head is covered with bruises caused by his mom.

You might have a hard time believing such families exist, but they do, and they are part of our reality. We live on the same planet and our realities can be completely different. But we can still see what is happening around us and learn valuable lessons, trying to make changes, without causing any additional harm. Who am I to say what is good and what is wrong? Almost everything is relative, and we operate on so many different perceptions, but I will abide to the global consciousness. I rely on human compassion and acknowledge that I am not here to change one's judgement, but to observe and speak up when injustice occurs.

All those with a higher consciousness should fight for better education, including when it comes to young people. The current educational system is failing all over the world, because of the hidden selfish agenda behind it. We need people like Socrates, Aristotle, and Marcus Aurelius as part of our educational system. I'm not saying that such people don't exist anymore. They are present, but they must be allowed to speak out with ease, as they might contribute to the morals and virtues necessary for the future generations.

Two thousand years ago, they would have taught young people how to behave in society and how to treat others. They might have held lessons on compassion and the virtues of life, teaching them to always tell the truth and be a true human with a spine. The agenda of today is different. Kids are taught to choose their sexuality from a young age, instead of being guided towards adulthood, like humanity has done in the past thousands of years without any problems. Future generations are pushed by an invisible but strong force into taking decisions that do not belong to them. Their creativity and innocence are affected. They are turning into teenagers who must deal with emotional imbalance. The situation is worse than ever, especially since the educational system has started to create its own agenda behind closed doors.

If we have even the tiniest seed of understanding, we can see through the bullshit that we are fed, social media, television, radios, newspapers, and other sources of information have a great influence on the world. It is up to us to come together once more, to be united, to educate and rebalance the level of consciousness on our planet. It is time that we take back our power and recreate the nourishing lands that were once filled with joy and abundance. Just like Charlie Chaplin said almost a hundred years ago: "And the power they took from the people, shall return to the people".

There is nothing worse than a dispersed society, where self-hate is promoted, and differences are made obvious. Living in such a society, chances are that we will forget how we are all one. We are now at the point where we hate each other because of our colour, sexual orientation, or culture. This has been going on for too many years, but no more. Our consciousness is changing, and we become more aware of such things. We all have the possibility to connect with our compassionate self. As a result, understanding each other becomes easier.

No matter where we are from and how we look like, no matter if we have disabilities or anything else that differentiate us from others, at the end of the day, we are one true spirit, living a human experience. We are all sons and daughters of Mother Earth. I call our planet Mother Earth because it has been nourishing us for so long, without any judgement, even if we keep making mistakes, burning its forests, and using our ego for selfish personal benefits. The father, if you will, lives on the outside of the planet. I am talking about the universe, which teaches us lessons from a distance, just like a father would. It lets us make mistakes over and over, until we learn them. Our father is in the sky above and the Earth is our mother. We are the sons and daughters sent to learn, grow, and evolve.

Try to define your legacy. Think about what this word means to you and what kind of impact you want to have in this world. Is there anything you would like to be remembered for? If yes, what values do you want to pass on? By the end of this chapter, I hope that you will be able to at least underline what matters to you the most in life. Take a pen and a sheet of paper, and do the following exercise, as this will help you determine your values. You can call it "My values".

Start by determining what values are most important to you, think long and hard about what makes you tick. Potential values include integrity, kindness, friendship, compassion, hard work, and discipline. Make a list with at least five values that you stand by, the ones that represent you the most. Everyone has at least these five main values. We have about twelve universal core values: unity, love and caring, respect, tolerance, peace, honesty, humility, happiness, cooperation, responsibility, simplicity, and freedom.

You can identify yours by asking yourself a few questions. First, think of the moments that were the most important in your life. What made them matter to you? And what about the opposite, what made you click on the negative side? What makes you feel angry? Imagine your ideal world, your own personal utopia. What does that look like?

Take your time and travel further into your memories. Remember, imagine, touch, and feel whatever you can, so that you can digest everything with ease. Find the past and present experiences that determine you values. Do not rush, take notes, and ask yourself whether your values are real, or they represent imposed beliefs, either by parents or society. Don't do it all in five minutes, your personality is much more complex than you might think, you cannot break it down in two or three phrases. Take a piece of paper and keep writing on it, every day of the week, for as long as you think it is necessary. Leave it on your desk or another table in your home. Write on it as much as you think you should.

Remember that there is no such thing as right or wrong when it comes to choosing what you want to do in life. And there is no shame regarding the choices you will decide to make. A carpenter cannot be compared to a music creator, and we will not compare an apple tree with a banana tree either. They all have their benefits, bringing a certain type of joy to the world. A carpenter can create marvellous furniture, wood carvings, and many other creative works. He will enjoy his own work, bringing wonder to the world with his talent. The music creator has his own creativity, which also brings joy to the world. Just think of the amazing sounds he might produce.

Try to look at things from a different perspective. On this planet, we are all part of a grand orchard and each one of us bears his own fruits, which benefit us all. No matter what area you chose to bloom in, there will always be someone out there who will benefit from your work or passion. All you need to do is identify your weakness and turn it into a strength. Turn it into your passion, so that later it will benefit your community, family, or friends.

Once you have found your legacy, set yourself some high goals, which resonate with your core values and will have a positive impact on the world. Develop a plan of action and work on it, because working hard on your passion is not that hard as you might expect. We rarely get tired from doing something that we love. Take cocaine or heroin users for example, addiction is their number one priority, even if they know it is wrong. If you would have asked me back then about it, my answer might have been similar. That is why you must be careful and choose the right things to wish for.

In other words, you should choose your passion wisely. Otherwise, it will end up having a negative effect on your life. Your passion can turn into a life-destroying habit, which can affect your future, causing those around you to suffer as well. Let me give you can example. Let's say that you chose to become an MMA fighter and you became good at it, mastering all the skills and moves. If you wanted to become a fighter because you have been bullied and now you want to fight so that you can take your revenge on others, well that right there, is a recipe for failure. I mean look at the police officers who become cops just because they were bullied as kids. They are after revenge and nothing more. Just look at the George Floyd incident from 2020 and many others around the world.

You want to become a master of martial arts to harness your strength and gain the wisdom that comes with it, not to conquer the world for selfish and insecure reasons. You might be able to fight several people at once, but you are wise enough to understand that fighting is not always the solution. The key lies in understanding your strength. You are choosing not to fight, having discovered the meaning of a true warrior. As a wise person once said, in becoming the master of your emotions, you will gain true freedom.

Let me tell you the story of the Japanese master and the samurai warrior.

"Long ago, near Tokyo, lived an old and respected samurai who had won many battles. His time of fighting wars had passed. This wise samurai devoted himself to teaching young people. Everyone knew him, he was a legend. Despite his age, he could still defeat any opponent, no matter how strong the other person might have been. On a summer evening, a warrior known for his arrogance and little cavalry came to his home. He was famous for his provocative character and the lack of scruples. His strategy was to provoke the opponent until that person, moved by anger, lowered his guard and attacked blindly. It was said that he had never been defeated.

In that afternoon, he was about to destroy the legend of the old samurai, to further increase his fame. The warrior began to insult the wise samurai, throwing stones at him and even spitting in his face. The minutes and hours passed, but the wise samurai remained impassive, refusing to pull his sword out. In the evening, exhausted and humiliated, the warrior called for victory. The disciples of the samurai were annoyed by his behaviour. How could he accept the insults of the warrior? They did not understand why the old man had not defended himself and considered his attitude a sign of cowardice.

So, they asked him:

– Master, how could you endure such unworthiness? Why didn't you pull your sword, knowing that you were going to lose the battle, rather than act in such a vile way?

The master replied:

– If someone comes with a gift and you do not accept it, who does the gift belong to?

– To the person who came to deliver it!

– Well, the same applies to anger, insults, and envy. When these are not accepted, they continue to belong to those who have brought them."

This is a great lesson on how to respond when provoked. You should educate yourself not to react to life's adversities. We need to be in alignment with our passion and use it to our benefit. Think hard about what you wish to become, because you never know how great you will become at it and how it can affect the world. At the end of the day, your choices have been made, under the best of your abilities at the time that those actions have been taken.

"In becoming the master of your emotions, you will gain true freedom". Unknown Author

Personal development program sample – beginner level, Monday to Friday, by Adrian Vallace

WAKE UP TIME	TO DO	NOTES
6 to 6.30		

6.30 to 7		
7 to 7.30		
7.30 to 8		
8 to 8.15		
8 to 9		
8 to 9		
9 to 17		
13 to 14		

18 to 18.30		
18.30 to 20		
18.30 to 20		
20 to 21		
21 to 21.30		
21.30 to 22		

Personal development program sample - intermediate level, Monday to Friday, by Adrian Vallace

WAKE UP TIME	TO DO	NOTES

5 to 5.30		
5.30 to 6		
6 to 6.30		
6.30 to 7		
7 to 8		
7 to 8		
8 to 17		
13 to 14		
17 to 18		
18 to 19		
19 to 20		

19 to 20		
20 to 21		
21 to 22		
22 to 22.30		

Personal development program sample – advanced level, Monday to Friday, by Adrian Vallace.

WAKE UP TIME	TO DO	NOTES

4 to 4.30		
4.30 to 5.30		
5.30 to 6		
6 to 6.45		
6.45 to 7		
7 to 8		
7 to 8		
8 to 17		
13 to 14		

17 to 18		
18 to 18.30		
18.30 to 20		
18.30 to 20		
20 to 21		
21 to 22		
22 to 22.30		

Once you have found a balance in your daily routine, which should cover at least the essentials – physical, mental, and emotional health; finances; relationships; career; contribution to society – all will fall into place. The universe will get out of your way, and you will be able to create your own path. Always remember that a disciplined consistency represents the key to a successful life.

Personal development schedule sample – Saturday

WAKE UP TIME	TO DO	NOTES

7 to 7.30		
7.30 to 8.30		
8.30 to 9		
9 to 10		
10 to 11		
11 to 15		
15 to 16		

16 onwards free time to do whatever you want		
Try not to sleep later than midnight to keep your body balanced		

Personal development schedule sample - Sunday

WAKE UP TIME	TO DO	NOTES
8 to 8.30		
8.30 to 9.30		
9.30 to 10		
10 to 11		
11 to 12		
12 onwards free time to do whatever you want		

All afternoon		
22.00 Try to be in bed by ten so that you're ready for the following week.		

  I know this might be a harsh schedule, but if you summon the courage to get through a couple of months, I bet you will see major changes and improvements in your health, focus, and emotional balance. If you have managed to persevere for a month or two, challenge yourself to push through, for six months, then one year. Should you not like what you've become within a year, just drop it. But at least this much you owe to yourself, to see how much you can grow in a year by being disciplined. After that, you can turn it into a lifestyle of your choice.